FAITH A. OYEDEPO

GW00683456

MARRIAGE COVENANT

Marriage Covenant

Copyright © 1988 by:

Faith A. Oyedepo

Reprinted in 1993, 1994, 1998, 2008, 2009

2010 reprint

ISBN 978-2480-13-4

Published in Nigeria by:

DOMINION PUBLISHING HOUSE

For further information or permission, write:

DOMINION PUBLISHING HOUSE

Canaan Land, Km 10,Idiroko Road, Ota.

P.M.B. 21688, Ikeja, Lagos,

Nigeria.Tel: 234-1-7747546-8

Web: ww.davidoyedepoministries.org; www.faithoyedepo.org;

E-mail: dph@davidoyedepoministries.org

All Scripture quotations are from

the King James Version of the Bible, except otherwise stated.

Contents

Foreword		5
Marriage, A Garden		6
Introduction		7

Part I

Chapter 1:	What Marriage Is	9
Chapter 2:	Marriage Covenant	11
Chapter 3:	A Garden Of Treasure	19
Chapter 4:	The Relevance Of Marriage To The Church	39

Part II

Chapter 5:	God's Concept Of Marriage	47
Chapter 6:	Purpose Of Marriage	61

Part III

Chapter 7:	How To Find A Marriage Partner	97
Chapter 8:	Courtship	95
Chapter 9:	Planning For Marriage	103

Part IV

Chapter 10:	Family Government	113
Chapter 11:	Child Training	129
Chapter 12:	Sustaining The Christian Home	137
Chapter 13:	Relationship With The In-Laws	145
Chapter 14:	Getting Your Loved Ones Saved	149
Chapter 15:	Homo-sexuality: God's View And His Remedy	157
	Final Word	162

DEDICATION

To my darling husband, Rt. Rev. (Dr.) David O. Oyede-po, the greatest and best man in the world; David Jnr. and Isaac—my wonderful sons, Love and Joys—my precious daughters,who have all made marriage and family life fulfilling for me.

FOREWORD

Having gone through "Marriage Covenant", I am persuaded that marriage has more to offer than any living person has yet experienced. Its treasures are as diverse as they are many; but it takes conscious effort to dig out the treasures and profit by them.

Remarkable in its presentation of marriage as a garden of treasure, I believe that both partners, joined together in the marriage covenant, should read this dynamite prayerfully and with an aim to improve upon their relationship.

By the inspiration of the Holy Spirit, it is not out of place to say that virtually all aspects of marriage have been highlighted in this book. I highly recommend *Marriage Covenant* ; it is *fantastic!*

Rt. Rev. (Dr.) David O. Oyedepo

Marriage, A Garden

1

Marriage, a garden
Planted by God
For man and woman
Made in His image
Man to head
Woman to help

2

Marriage, a garden
A garden for two
To woo and be won
To love and to hold
To care and to cherish
To assist and uphold

3

Marriage, a garden
For peace not war
For pleasure not pressure
For attraction not distraction
For comfort not discomfort
For trust not distrust

4

Marriage, a garden
God's Word abides
God's treasure abides
God's love abides
God's beauty abides
God's glory abides

5

Marriage, a garden
A garden of teaching
A garden of learning
A garden of understanding
A garden of accommodating
A garden of appreciating

6

Marriage, a garden
Not for destruction
Not for defilement
Not for unfaithfulness
Not for hypocrites
Not for liars

7

Marriage, a garden
God's true garden
God the Author
God the planter
God the watcher
God the centre

Introduction

It has become necessary to update the work done in Marriage Covenant, not because the essential issues discussed in the book have become obsolete, but because we live in a dynamic world, which is prone to changes. As societies become more complex, marriage, as an institution, is affected. The world we live in is a press-button world of quick results—a jet age, and anything that does not produce at the touch of a button is disregarded. Marriage is not left out as well.

However, we see that marriage is much more than that. God's original plan was for man to leave his parents and cleave (permanently) to his wife. If man is not experiencing fulfilment in marriage, it is not because God did not create it to be fulfilling, but because man has left God out of marriage. And we know that it is only what God does that holds a guarantee of abiding forever (Eccl. 3:14).

Marriage is gold, and like most precious metals, one must invest time and resources to secure it and fashion it into a jewel of great price. Hebrews 3:4 says:

7

For every house is builded by some man; but he that built all things is God.

Since God built marriage, He has created all that it would take to make it work. Man on his own part needs to abide by God's principle and implement His plan. God has said:

Husbands, love your wives.

and to the woman He said:

Wives, submit yourselves unto your own husband.
Ephesians 5:25 and 22

If the man and the woman want to experience the gold in marriage, they must do as God says, without circumventing His laid down rules.

If marriage is a necessary evil, it is so because man has thought to push God out of it and do it himself. However, any one (man or woman alike) who will go by God's plan, will experience God's desired result; and his marriage will be sweet and fulfilling.

PART I

Chapter 1

What Marriage Is

Marriage is the oldest institution in the world and it has its root in divinity. God Himself instituted it.

> *...the Lord God...made...a woman, and brought her unto the man.*
>
> Genesis 2:22

It is the union, the coming together of two people of opposite sexes with a view to building a God-centred home. Notice the words, "woman" and "man" in the above scripture. Marriage is an honourable thing with the bed undefiled.

It is a unique relationship ordained by God, for a man and a woman to give and receive satisfaction for their healthy needs and desires. The relationship is unique because it involves the two individuals, spirit, soul and body. Spiritually, their lives must have been transformed, both of them being born-again, becoming new creatures and therefore, belonging to the same spiritual kingdom. In the realm of the soul, both of them should have the same mind concerning various matters, especially the principles of the doctrine of Christ as stated in Hebrews 6:1-2, for two cannot walk together except they be agreed (Amos 3:3). In the realm of the body, both must accept the fact that their bodies belong to each other and thus be ready to share it with one another.

Scripturally, this union is for a life time. It should, therefore, not be entered into unadvisedly. It is important to know what marriage is all about before one says "I do" to anyone.

Marriage is not peculiar to any culture or country of the world. It is heaven's culture. It is therefore not traditional in any way, but scriptural. God's Word gives us guidance on what needs to be known about it in order to make it successful.

Since marriage was instituted by God Himself, anyone who wants success in marriage should make God the centre of such a relationship. God is the only sure foundation for success in marriage.

Chapter 2

Marriage Covenant

Marriage Is A Covenant, Not A Promise

Marriage is a covenant relationship, not a promise. A covenant is different from just a promise. A promise is a verbal or written undertaking, to do or not to do something. There are no conditions attached to it. A covenant is, however, a formal contractual agreement between two or more parties, with each party agreeing to do something as a prerequisite to receiving some benefits. A breach of the agreement by any party disqualifies him from reaping the rewards and privileges attached to the covenant. A covenant is usually written, and sealed.

Many people, especially Christians, think that a good marriage is a promise from God, so they wait endlessly for the fulfilment of that promise. Others think it comes by wishing, so they keep wishing.

There is an adage that says, "If wishes were horses,

beggars would ride." A good home and marriage is not a promise from God, neither does it come by wishing. Marriage is a covenant.

The marriage covenant involves two parties: God on one hand and the man (and his wife) on the other. God is the initiator of the covenant and His terms of agreement are sealed up in His Word. Man on his part is required to obey God's terms of the agreement as stated in harmony, abundance and fulfilment in the home.

God's side of the covenant is constant because He is invariable and faithful.

> *For I am the Lord, I change not.*
>
> Malachi 3:6

God will always fulfil His own side of the covenant. The man (and his wife) who are the second party in the marriage covenant are the variables. They must be ready to obey the terms of agreement as stated in God's Word, so they can reap the rewards that go with obedience. Disobedience to God will make these blessings elusive.

The disobedience of man (and his wife) to the terms of the covenant as stated in God's Word is usually the cause of many marital sorrows, problems, frustration and eventual divorce.

The Terms Of The Covenant

Marriage is a legal contract involving two people: the man and his wife. Each one has to fulfil his own part of the covenant, if they are to enjoy the best that marriage has to offer. What is the man's responsibility? It is to govern the home and cater for the needs of his family (this includes spiritual, physical and material needs). Ephesians 5:23 says,

> *For the husband is the head of the wife, even as Christ is the head of the Church.*

And again, 1 Timothy 5:8 says,

> *But if any provide not for his own, and specially for those of his own house, he hath denied the faith, and is worse than an infidel.*

What is the woman's role in this covenant?

Ephesians 5:22 sums it up this way:

> *Wives, submit yourselves unto your own husbands, as unto the Lord.*

In essence, if the man and his wife are to experience fulfilment in marriage, then they must adhere to the terms of this marriage covenant.

What is God's own role in the covenant? Hebrews 3:4 states:

For every house is builded by some man, but he that built all things is God.

God assures us that if, as man and wife, man fulfils his own responsibility and builds his home, He will ensure that his home remains built, guaranteeing fulfilment for every member of the home.

The terms of the covenant as it relates to the man and his wife are discussed in detail in the chapter on family government.

Obey The Terms Of The Covenant

If ye be willing and obedient, ye shall eat the good of the land.

Isaiah 1:19

Many people want to eat the fruit of a happy home but are not ready to be obedient to the terms of the covenant. This cannot happen. Outside of obedience, the fruit of a good home cannot be obtained. A good home is therefore the fruit of obedience. A good, fulfilled marriage is a possibility, but only those that are ready to obey the terms of the agreement can have access to this unique fruit. There are some obedient individuals that are presently eating the fruit of a good, fulfilled marriage.

You can join the company if you wish. God is no

respecter of persons. If you will be obedient like others, what others are enjoying you can also enjoy. Marriage is meant to be sweet, enjoyable and failure-proof, if only couples will obey the terms of the covenant as stated in God's Word.

You Are The Builder Of Your Home

For every house is builded by some man; but he that built all things is God.

Hebrews 3:4

Marriage can be likened to a physical house. Houses in the physical don't just happen, they are consciously built. You don't just wake up one day and see a fully built physical house somewhere. It takes conscious effort and input to make it happen. In the same manner, and even much more, a good marriage doesn't just happen; it is consciously made to happen!

An individual who wants to enjoy a good marriage must be ready to make it happen. You are the architect of your own marriage. Whether a marriage succeeds or not is determined by the man (and his wife) who are the variable factors. The destiny of a marriage is in the hands of the couple themselves; a clear proof can be seen in I Corinthians 3:21, which says that *"all things are yours."*

Consciously and resolutely work out the destination of your home. No one else can build your home for you; you have the duty to build it the way you want it. Stop shifting your responsibilities to God. The act of building is your responsibility. You must fulfil your own part for God to fulfil His own.

Your Marriage Is What You Make It

The law of creation forbids things happening by themselves, they must be made to happen.

> *...God created the heaven and the earth.*
>
> Genesis 1:1

> *Thus saith the Lord, The heaven is my throne, and the earth is my footstool...*
>
> Isaiah 66:1

The heaven, which is God's throne, and the earth, His footstool, were created by Him in the beginning. He had to first create (make to be) the heaven and the earth before He could dwell therein. The same way, you can make a heaven of your home here on earth. However, the home and marriage you will enjoy must, of a necessity, be created by you. Your marriage is what you make it to be. Stop waiting for your home to adjust itself, rather adjust it with the Word of God.

After God created the heaven and the earth, suddenly,

...the earth was without form, and void...

Genesis 1:2

God did not just keep silent, watching; He acted and reshaped the world to what He desired, and only then did He see that everything was very good. Is your marriage "without form and void?" Do not keep silent watching it, act and make it what it ought to be. You can do it! You are a co-creator with God your Father. Your situation is not beyond repair. Act on the Word of God and see your home become a heaven on earth.

He That Built All Things *Is* God

True, you are the builder of your home, but remember that God is the ultimate builder. Constantly remember that you are only able to keep your home through God's enablement. The Word of God is the basic raw material required for effective building. As you keep applying the raw materials and your home is being built, don't forget to give all the glory back to God. After all,

...without Me (Jesus) ye can do nothing.

John 15:5

Never give room to pride in your life when you start seeing the good fruit of a blessed marriage. Pride is a destroyer of man's destiny; so, give it no place. Attribute whatever goodness you see in your home to

God and Him alone. As you keep lifting Him up even in your home, you will experience more of more of Him.

Chapter 3

A Garden Of Treasure

Garden

A garden typifies pleasure, abundance, and fulfilment.
Marriage can be likened to a garden. The Oxford Dic-
tionary defines garden as a piece of ground used for
growing things such as flowers, fruit, vegetables, etc.
The marriage garden was planted by God Himself.
There is a very fascinating story in Genesis 2:8-16.

...the Lord God planted a garden...

Verse 8

God Himself is the great planter of this garden and
you can be sure that His design is the best. The maximum yield of a physical garden is determined by the
use to which it is put and how well it is taken care of.
The marriage garden operates this way too. Put this
garden to the best use and you will get a maximum

yield from it and if you take proper care of it, the output will be affected positively.

Treasure

Marriage is not just an ordinary garden, but a garden full of treasures. Treasures are highly valued objects, which when profitably traded with, take one off the realm of the ordinary to that of the supernatural. They also raise one from the realm of poverty to riches. In the same way, when the treasures in marriage are properly harnessed, one is bound to enjoy success.

However, most treasures are buried deep inside the earth and have to be dug out before they can be of any use. You must believe that those treasures are there and then consciously dig them out, before you can profit by them. I am a living witness and testimony to the fact that the marriage garden is full of treasures.

By the grace of God, I have already started digging out some of the treasures in it, and I tell you, they are profitable. God is no respecter of persons, the same Lord is rich unto all. You can also start digging out the treasures and make use of them to the glory of God.

Digging

The act of digging is a process and it requires labour,

diligence, wisdom, determination, patience and time, among other things. Many people don't want to dig, but want to enjoy the treasures. There can be no achievement without demand. The strength required for digging will be supplied to you by God Himself.

Digging, to know the one you are married to, is a must. We must study and understand our spouses. Proverbs 24:3 says:

> *Through wisdom is an house builded; and by understanding it is established.*

If you want an established and fulfilled home, you must utilize the tool of understanding to dig into your spouse. Remember, what your home becomes is determined by how much you have invested in digging up its treasures. You can become a blessing to your generation via your home.

Let us examine some of the treasures in the marriage garden.

1. Trees

Out of the ground made the Lord God to grow every tree that is pleasant to the sight, and good for food...
Genesis 2:9

One of the assets in the marriage garden planted by God are trees. In the natural, trees have several uses and can be converted into several other useful things. Firstly, well planted trees are a thing of beauty and they beautify the environment. That is why the scripture says,

...every tree that is pleasant to the sight...

Marriage is also meant to be beautiful! You can enjoy the beauty of marriage if you choose to.

Secondly, trees provide shade from the heat of the sun and are used to prevent desert encroachment. Your marriage can be shielded from the heat of the scourging sun, that is beating many people so hard in the world today. Deserts talk about dryness, thirst and hunger. Your home is not created to suffer any of these. So if you will walk in accordance with God's Word, you will be exempted.

Thirdly, certain trees in the natural are used in draining excessive water from swampy areas. Marriage is meant to help you curtail the excesses of life. Swampy areas breed mosquitoes and cause health hazards. All hazards of life can be taken care of by your consciously obeying what the scriptures say about marriage.

Fourthly, some trees bear edible fruits.

Out of the ground made the Lord God to grow every tree that is...good for food...

Marriage is meant to give you satisfaction in life. Don't die of hunger when you can be filled. Many in the world are dying (even though married), for lack of fulfilment. It is hunger or a lack of fulfilment in marriage that makes a married man or woman go outside the home to commit adultery. Begin to tap into the treasures in marriage and enjoy God's best for your life.

Fifthly, trees can be converted into several other useful things, such as paper, firewood, rubber; and from trees, houses are also built. If the resources in marriage are profitably tapped, they make you a man and woman of many parts. You become useful in many areas of life. An understanding of this truth has helped me to diversify in many areas of my life, and made me to become a blessing to more people than I ever thought. You can do the same.

2. River

And a river went out of Eden to water the garden.
Genesis 2:10

Another treasure found in the garden planted by God is the river. Rivers are of tremendous benefit to man. From them, you get water for drinking, bathing and washing purposes. Rivers can also be used for irrigation, making all-year-round farming possible.

Don't die of thirst in your marriage when there are lots of thirst-quenching rivers in it. It is thirst in marriage that makes couples prefer staying away from home, rather than enjoying their homes with their families. I know of a man who prefers to stay back in the office after closing hours, rather than go home. It is not because he has work to do, but so as to keep away from home and have some peace. The home atmosphere was not what it ought to be. You can purpose to make the atmosphere in your home the best for the Holy Spirit, as well as for your spouse and children.

To the glory of God, my husband and I receive a lot of inspiration from the Holy Spirit right inside our home. More often than not, a greater percentage of instructions we have received for our ministry to date were received right at home. Make the atmosphere of your home a conducive one.

You can dam a river for hydro-electric power supply. Over 90% of the electricity power supply in Nigeria to date is generated from only one source - River Niger. What a source of power! In the same way, when you tap into God's resources in marriage, your home becomes a tremendous source of spiritual power supply, not just for yourself, but for others and the body of

Christ at large. No wonder Ecclesiastes 4:9 maintains that, *"Two are better than one."*

Moreover, the river is also a bank for all kinds of treasures. All kinds of mineral deposits can be found in the river bed. But they are not just found on the surface of the river. You have to dig deep down. These minerals, when profitably traded with, bring great returns and thereby prosper you. That is why Isaiah 60:5 says,

> *...The abundance of the sea shall be converted unto thee...*

When you handle marriage the scriptural way, you are bound to prosper in all areas of your life.

Dressing And Keeping The Garden

> *And the Lord God took the man, and put him into the garden of Eden to dress it and to keep it.*
>
> Genesis 2:15

God put man (male and female; husband and wife) into the garden for two reasons: first, to dress it, and second, to keep it.

Dressing a garden simply means caring for it. When dressing a garden, you remove all unwanted elements, such as weeds. You water it and put manure in it so the yield can be high. Labour, time, diligence, patience, among other things, are involved. When you dress the garden, you make it beautiful and its productivity is increased. It is the same thing with marriage.

For you to enjoy the best of it, it is your duty to make it fit. Don't be too lazy, selfish, careless or indifferent. Invest spiritual labour in prayer, study of the Word, sharing and diligently apply the virtue of patience and see what God will do.

It is not enough to dress your marriage garden without keeping it. Keeping the garden means protection, giving it a covering, avoiding any exposure to danger. If a garden is well dressed but is not kept, any destroyer can have access to it ;and in a moment all the labour spent on it will be destroyed. Your home is for keeps. It should be shielded from the enemy, who is the destroyer. No matter how well you dress a garden, as long as it is not kept, it shall be thrown down and trodden upon.

The garden you cannot dress, you will not keep. Adam dressed but did not keep his garden; no wonder the devil was able to come in and cause damage. Shield your home from the attacks of the enemy; be concerned about the company your spouse keeps, his/her likes and dislikes, his/her movements, etc. Keep your garden or else after your spouse has been beguiled, you will also be affected. As you do your own part in dressing and keeping the garden, trust in the Lord absolutely for, *"Except the Lord keep the city, the watchman waketh but in vain"* (Psalms 127:1).

God has mapped out a course for both the man and his wife to follow, if they intend to enjoy the gold in the land.

And the gold in that land is good.

Genesis 2:12

But to tap the best the land has to offer, there is a condition attached.

If ye be willing and obedient, ye shall eat the good of the land.

Isaiah 1:19

The man and his wife have to be willing to obey the instructions of the Lord, as well as purposefully obey them.

God's Instruction To The Man

A tool has been given to the man, with which to cultivate his marriage garden. It is so effective that if the man uses it diligently, and according to direction, he will dig out the treasures in the marriage garden. This instrument is so vital that God Himself used it to draw man back to Himself. It is something the world sings about, talks about and really longs for -

but something which they do not have because it is of God. What is that tool? It is love. The Bible, talking about God, said,

> *...God so loved the world that he gave His only begotten Son, that whosoever believeth in Him should not perish, but have everlasting life.*

John 3:16

If God could employ love to win the whole of humanity to Himself, and has instructed man (the head of the home) to employ the same tool, then man should, because it is of great profit. Ephesians 5:25 gives a definite command:

> *Husbands, love your wives, even as Christ also loved the Church, and gave Himself for it.*

The God-type of love is unconditional. Jesus loved the Church when there was no Church yet. He died for wicked man; His love was not as a result of our love for Him. He loved us so much, He paid the greatest price any one could ever pay; He laid down His life.

> *Hereby perceive we the love of God, because He laid down His life for us.*

1 John 3:16

The only type of love that can stand the test of time and that can dig out the treasures in the garden, is the

God-kind of love, unconditional love. There is no woman who does not respond to love. Even if she does not respond at first, keep loving her and very soon you will be amazed at the warmth and closeness it will generate.

Love must be expressed. It must be shown. When one loves another, it is so obvious by the things he says, does and even thinks. The depth of love one has for another is seen in its expression. God, who is our perfect example, so loved the world that He gave His Son. His love was expressed in His giving. Jesus so loved us that He laid down His life. Let us together look at the lives of certain men who loved the Lord and expressed it.

Abraham loved the Lord and demonstrated this by preparing his only son, Isaac, for a burnt offering unto the Lord. He was so steadfast in his love that only God could call out from heaven to stop him from slaying the boy. Not even the cry of Isaac or the agony of Sarah if she found out, could deter him from carrying out God's commands to the letter. He was so total in his commitment to God. How would God have known that Abraham loved Him more than Isaac, if he had not demonstrated it in the way he did? Solomon also had this testimony.

And Solomon loved the Lord...

1 Kings 3:3

His love was not complete until he had expressed it. What did he do as an expression of his love?

And the king went to Gibeon to sacrifice there...a thousand burnt offerings did Solomon offer upon that altar.

verse 4

Solomon gave a thousand burnt offerings! What an expression of love! In essence, genuine love cannot be suppressed; it must be expressed for it to achieve the desired results. So, how is love best expressed in marriage relationship?

(i) In Words

Words are powerful, and we are a product of words. Negative words produce pessimists, while positive words produce optimists, possibility thinkers and achievers. How forcible are right words! (Job 6:25). When God came down to create the earth, what He saw was enough discouragement: He saw a world without form, void, and covered with darkness. He did not despair; instead, He spoke His heart's desire. To dispel the darkness, He called forth light; and to give form to the shapeless earth, He made a firmament, divided the waters and gradually what was shapeless, hopeless and seemingly useless became a thing to behold.

In expressing his love, the husband must consciously ignore the negative, unattractive things about his wife and say the positive. He must express his love through the things he says about and to his wife. He must always tell her how much he loves her, how much she means to him, how he loves the way she does certain things, etc. With time, he will discover that she begins to measure up to his expectations. If he calls her a virtuous woman, she will long to live up to that title. The faith she needs to become all the things he says she is, comes as she constantly hears them. Romans 10:17 caps it up.

So then faith cometh by hearing, and hearing by the Word of God.

ii. Actions And Attitudes

Do you know that when your action matches your declaration, there is a fortification of your association? It is true. You see, one declares his love for his wife, then matches his declaration with positive actions. What results is a strengthening or a fortification of that association. If you are a husband, and you say you love your wife, go ahead and prove it by the things you do and the steps you take.

Express your love, look out for her welfare, notice new things about her, buy her gifts from time to time. In essence, cherish her, nourish her and ravish her with your love. It is not unmanly to demonstrate your love in your actions and attitudes. Don't criticise or ridicule her; don't make her feel there is nothing she knows how to do. Encourage and motivate her to be her best for God.

Though used in a different context, I believe James 1:22 fits into all that this section is trying to say:

But be ye doers of the Word...

Take a step further by doing or demonstrating what you have said. Actions truly speak louder than words. In John 15:14 Jesus said,

Ye are my friends, if ye do whatsoever I command you.

If you cannot do God's command, then you are not His friend. And if you are not His friend, what are you but His enemy?

There is no short-cut; if you love your wife, demonstrate it, because love is not love until it is expressed. In essence, the tools for dressing and keeping the garden are available. All the husband needs to do to fulfils his own role is to receive grace to love his wife in word and indeed.

God's Instruction To The Woman

Much talked about but far from being fully under-stood, is the issue of submission—the God-given re-sponsibility to the woman. God did not make the woman inferior; in fact, before the fall, He saw both the man and his wife as equals. But when the woman yielded to the suggestion of the devil, God's verdict was:

> *...Thy desire shall be to thy husband, and he shall rule over thee.*
>
> Genesis 3;16

Before the fall, the man did not have to lord it over his wife, because they were naturally of one mind. It was the fall which provoked God's pronouncements. When Christ came, He redeemed the man and the woman from God's judgment and released grace for the wife to submit to her husband. In case the woman is in doubt as to whether that command is still in force or not, God reiterated it in Ephesians 5:22,

> *Wives, submit yourselves unto your own husbands, as unto the Lord.*

Though no longer under the curse, the woman is still expected to submit to the man. He is still placed over her.

The wonderful thing about obeying God and genuinely submitting to one's husband, is that automatically, there is a covering over such a woman. There is now one to protect her, one to fend for her, one to look after her. The stubborn self-willed woman is at a loss, because the care she should naturally enjoy from the man is simply not there. Ecclesiastes 4:9-12 outlines some of the benefits of submitting to the man.

i. Submission Fosters Unity

When the woman submits to her husband, she finds that they are working together. In love, he instructs her on what to do and how to go about it and she, in submission carries it out to the letter. The idea works and they both are excited ands have a good reward for their labour.

> *Two are better than one; because they have a good reward for their labour.*
>
> Verse 9

ii. Submission Provokes Genuine Care

The woman that submits to her husband makes it easy for him to care for her. She entrusts him with her life, so to say, and he, by God's grace desires to cater for her every need. Because of the symbiotic relationship, one finds that the woman watches out for the

34

welfare of her husband. If he falls, she is there to raise him up. Likewise, when she is weak, he pulls her up to the place of strength in God.

For if they fall, the one will lift up his fellow: but woe to him that is alone when he falleth; for he hath not another to help him up.

Verse 10

A rebellious and unsubmissive woman is alone. She struggles to take decisions on her own and to execute them. In political terms, she is both the legislature (the one with the power to make and change laws) and the executive (person who carries out what has been planned or decided)! Such a woman has removed her covering and should expect unprecedented attacks.

iii. Submission Brings A Covering

Verse 11 of Ecclesiastes 4 says:

Again, if two lie together, then they have heat: but how can one be warm alone?

When two lie together to keep warm, their arms may be wrapped around each other. Before an attacker can penetrate into one, he must pass through the other. Before a man of God yields to temptation, most times, there is a vacuum created by his wife. A rebellious, unyielding woman opens her home up to attacks. If a woman is submissive to her husband, people will begin to respect her. She may not trace it to the fact that she is submissive but it is. If she unconditionally submits inside, people outside will submit to her authority.

iv. No One Can Prevail Against Her

People find it difficult to insult married women. Why? Perhaps it is out of respect for her status or out of fear of her husband. As long as the woman is married, there is a covering that prevents people from insulting her. No wonder then that Ecclesiastes 4:12 says:

> *And if one prevail against him, two shall withstand him; and a threefold cord is not quickly broken.*

Who is the third party in the union of man and wife? It is God Himself!

Having outlined the benefits of submission, let me quickly say that submission, just like love, must be expressed. It is not enough to act submissive — a vital part of submission — but the thoughts of the heart and the words of the mouth must be submissive as well.

However, because submission flows from the heart, it cannot be faked for long; soon the true state of the heart will be exposed. But submission in the heart must show in the way the wife addresses her husband

and responds to his demands, especially when it is inconvenient for her. God's Holy Spirit wants to make submission easier for women. But women must die to self and be open to the leading of the Lord. That is why Ephesians 5:22 says:

Wives submit yourselves unto your own husbands as unto the Lord.

Our submission should first be unto the Lord and then submitting to our husbands won't be difficult.

Chapter 4

The Relevance Of Marriage To The Church

Marriage and the Church are interwoven, and are therefore, inseparable. Homes are built from marriages and the Church is made up of homes. The Church in this context refers to the Body of Christ. There is no way the Church can exist without homes. Marriage therefore becomes very relevant to the Church for certain reasons:-

1. Marriage Is The Bedrock Of The Church

Because marriage and the Church are inseparable, the state of one automatically affects the other. Healthy marriages mean healthy homes, and healthy homes make for a healthy Church; the opposite applies in an unhealthy marriage. Build up the home and the Church will be built.

To get the Church to her proper place, marriages must be put into proper shape. The Church cannot shy away from this fact any more. There is a need for believers to be exposed to God's concept of marriage through sound biblical teachings. The Church should not underestimate the importance of marriage, for Christ is coming for a Church without spot or wrinkle (Eph. 5:27).

If the Church must grow to maturity before Christ comes, then marriages must be strengthened. How strong the church is will be affected to a great extent, by how strong marriages are. There is therefore, the need to solidify marriages, so that the Church can grow to maturity.

2. Humanity Was Dethroned Through The Home

The devil dethroned humanity through the home:

...The serpent beguiled Eve through his subtlety...
II Corinthians 11:3

Therefore the Lord God sent him forth from the Garden of Eden...

Genesis 3:23

When things fell apart in the home, man was driven

out of the garden; he was dethroned. For humanity to be re-enthroned, the home must be what God has ordained it to be. If you, as an individual member of the body, do not want to suffer dethronement like Adam did, your home must be patterned after God and His Word. If there will be restoration to humanity, it has to come through the home.

3. Effectual Prayer Requires The Home Being In Order

After the institution of marriage, man began to enjoy fellowship with God. But after the fall, which came through the home, fellowship was lost. Thank God Jesus' coming brought restoration. However, for fellowship with God in prayers to be effective, the home must be in shape.

> *Likewise, ye husbands, dwell with them according to knowledge...as being heirs together of the grace of life; that your prayers be not hindered.*
>
> I Peter 3:7

Your home must be a successful one, for your prayers not to be hindered. Are you a prayer warrior? How is your home? If your home is not in order, do not bother yourself praying, because such prayers shall be hindered. I am glad to let you know that God does not answer prayers when they are hindered. Knowing very well the importance of prayer as Christians, it is important to put our homes in order, so that we can enjoy the full benefits of prayer.

Based on the afore-mentioned points, the importance of marriage to the Church cannot be over-emphasized. Let us join hands together to build the Church of Christ by building our homes.

Instances From God's Word

In times of old when Israel had kings, the state of the family either enhanced the affairs of the throne or militated against it. Solomon's heart departed from the Lord because he amassed strange women. I Kings 11:1-2 says:

But king Solomon Loved many strange women...

Of the nations concerning which the Lord said unto the children of Israel, Ye shall not go in to them, neither shall they come in unto you: for surely they will turn away your heart after their gods: Solomon clave unto these in love.

What was God's reaction to this? Verses 9 & 11:

And the Lord was angry with Solomon...

For as much as this is done of thee...

I will surely rend the kingdom from thee, and will give it to thy servant.

Solomon, the leader of Israel, lost his throne because his family life was not up to God's standard. In the same vein, shepherds in the Body of Christ must ensure that they discipline themselves and keep their own wives. A weakness in this area could be devastating.

Another man whose family life wrecked his career and ruined God's call upon his life was Samson. His love for strange women estranged him from God and finally put an abrupt end to his life. His parents had tried to constrain him, saying; *"Is there never a woman among the daughters of thy brethren...that thou goest to take a wife of the uncircumcised Philistines?"* (Judges 14:3). In a more recent story in the New Testament, and among the first century Christians, we see a marriage that was a blemish to the body (Acts 5:1-11).

Let us consider verse 9: *"Then Peter said unto her, How is it that ye have agreed together to tempt the Spirit of the Lord?"* And the consequence? *"Behold, the feet of them which have buried thy husband are at the door, and shall carry thee out."* Verse 10 further says: *"Then fell she down straightaway at his feet, and yielded up the ghost...And great fear came upon all the church."*

Maybe hitherto Ananias and Sapphira had been zealously serving the Body of Christ. However, a day came that they noticed that the disciples of Jesus were sowing in the Kingdom; and so as not to break the trend of their Kingdom service, they decided to give; but they both connived to falsify the sum of money they had received from selling the land. Their death was the first of its kind in the church and it instilled fear in the hearts of others. Their untimely death was a blow to the Body of Christ and could have been averted, if their marriage was responsive to the Holy Ghost.

However, there are marriages in the scriptures that are worthy of emulation. Abraham and Sarah are good examples of a perfect union. Abraham loved Sarah and she in turn, submitted herself to him. It was so much that she is cited as an example of submission in I Peter 3:5 & 6:

> *For after this manner in the old time the holy women also, who trusted in God, adorned themselves, being in subjection unto their own husbands:*

> *Even as Sarah obeyed Abraham, calling him Lord: whose daughters ye are, as long as ye do well, and are not afraid with any amazement.*

I believe it was possible for Abraham to show hospitality to strangers because he had a wife like Sarah, who would respond delightedly. How we need to emulate such a marriage!

Another couple noted for good works and hospitality is Aquila and Priscilla. They took Paul in. In fact,

Romans 16:3 says:

> *Greet Priscilla and Aquila my helpers in Christ*
> *Jesus.*

Their home was a succour to visitors and men of God. They even had a church in their house (I Cor. 16:19). These two, together, made their homes conducive for the Holy Ghost to operate in and bless lives. Anytime Paul saw someone going to Corinth, he sent a salutation to Aquila and Priscilla.

> *Salute Priscilla and Aquila...*
>
> 2 Timothy 4:19

The onus now rests on you to choose what type of home yours will be. It can either be a highlight or a blemish on the Church of Christ.

PART II

Chapter 5

God's Concept Of Marriage

There are always two concepts or views to every issue of life — God's and man's. And the two are always ever contrary to each other. The individual is expected to choose whether to accept God's concept or man's concept. God's concept will always bring fulfilment when followed, while man's concept will lead to a disastrous end.

This assertion is true of marriage, too. God's ways and thoughts are higher than man's; and His perceptions are perfect. It is by accepting and walking by God's own concept that one can find fulfilment in life. What is God's concept of marriage?

Marriage Is Good

God's concept about marriage is that it is GOOD and it is to be enjoyed. This concept is contrary to man's claims on marriage. Some people say "Marriage is a necessary evil." Others introduce a state of irony into this holy institution. They contend that the married are looking for a way of escape, while the unmarried are eager to get into it. This assertion is borne out of man's philosophy and the experience of those who have not found fulfilment in marriage. But neither philosophy nor experience is the truth; God's Word is.

God instituted marriage. After He finished His work, He *"...saw everything that He had made, and, behold it was very good"*(Gen. 1:31). God is good and nothing less than good proceeds from Him. If marriage is evil, God would not have initiated it.

Many people believe the ideas of men more than the Word of God; and it is a spiritual law that what you believe affects what you experience. It is a spiritual law that it shall be unto you, according to your faith. The fact that some people experience problems, defeat and failure in marriage does not mean that everybody else is having similar experiences. No experience is as strong as the Word of God; rather, all experiences should be judged in the light of the Word. Any experience that is contrary to the Word of God should be thrown away.

A woman once came to my husband for counselling.

She began by making a sweeping statement that every home has its own peculiar problem. My husband had to cut in to correct her and point out that there are exceptions. Having problems in the home is not the rule. That you are sick, for instance, does not mean that everybody else is sick. God intends that believers' homes be a heaven on earth, where they can enjoy the Kingdom of God and the abundance it has to offer.

Buttressing the fact that marriage is good, Paul says, *"Marriage is honourable in all..."* (Hebrews 13:4). If marriage is evil, it cannot at the same time be honourable. Since it is honourable, it cannot be evil. James also says that,

> **Every good gift and every perfect gift is from above, and cometh down from the Father of lights, with whom is no variableness, neither shadow of turning.**
>
> James 1:17

Since marriage was instituted by God, and God is from above, marriage therefore comes from above, and cannot be less than good. Marriage is not only good, it is perfect.

Scripturally, marriage is good. It is the use to which some put it that paints a deceptive picture of evil. Whatever man's concept you have heard about marriage, put it aside and believe what the Bible says about marriage, because this is the only authentic view. Ever before I got married, I already discovered and accepted God's concept of marriage, at the expense of man's concept, which has captured many men; and it is working for me. To the glory of God, I am not only enjoying the goodness in marriage, I am also moving towards the perfection in it. You can enjoy it also, because the same God is rich unto all and He is no respecter of persons!

Marriage Involves Leaving

In God's concept of marriage, both the man and the woman involved must be ready to leave their parents and relatives.

For this cause shall a man LEAVE his father and mother, and cleave to his wife.

Mark 10:7

The couple must be ready to detach themselves from parents and relatives. After marriage, you are not expected to be tied to the strings of your parents' aprons any longer. You must be able to gain and operate some degree of independence from your parents. You must be able to take some decisions by yourself and accept responsibility over your life and that of your spouse.

After marriage, you don't have to accept every counsel and instruction from parents and relations. All must be carefully weighed under the light of the Word and in the interest of your home. In case they are contrary to God's Word you are not obliged to follow them.

Some parents usually find it difficult to let go of their children. Some couples find it easy to report everything that happens in their homes to their parents and relations. This is a sign that such individuals have not followed God's laid down principle of leaving. This is the *raison d'etre* for the troubles in many homes today.

A woman once walked into my office for counselling. She said each time any of her husband's relations writes or visits them, the man was always quarrelling with her. Sometimes, the relationship will degenerate so low that the man will refuse to eat any food prepared by her. This is a clear proof that the man is still being remotely controlled by his relations. He puts at a premium the interest of his people over and above that of his own family. This is contrary to God's idea of marriage. If a couple can gain parental independence, then it will be easy to be free from the apron strings of relations.

Majority of the problems in homes today can be linked

directly or indirectly to this issue. Divorce is on the increase in Christendom, because the people of God have forsaken the instruction of God to the couple to "leave father and mother." There is no way to enjoy fulfilment in marriage without first leaving father and mother. This does not mean to abandon parents and have nothing to do with them any longer. Remember you are still expected to fulfil your roles as children to parents by caring for them. However, you must accept responsibility over your decisions and that of your spouse.

Marriage Involves Cleaving

For a marriage to be complete, a couple must not only leave father and mother, but also **cleave** to each other.

> *Therefore shall a man leave his father and his mother, and shall CLEAVE unto his wife...*
>
> Genesis 2:24

Each partner will leave parents to cleave to the other. "To cleave" means to be 'joined to.' When you compare Genesis 2:24 to Ephesians 5:31 'Cleave' is replaced with 'joined.'

The extent to which a couple is joined together, will be dictated by the extent to which they have detached themselves from the apron strings of their parents. There must first be a leaving before there can be a cleaving. Without cleaving, the couple cannot receive maximum joy, and benefits in marriage. When you cleave to your spouse as the scriptures recommend, nothing will be able to come between both of you.

Two Alone Make A Home

In God's concept of marriage, **two people alone** make a home. *"For this cause shall **a man** leave his father...and cleave to **his wife"** (Mark 10:7). A home is formed at the coming together of only two, not more. My darling husband says that when they are more than two, it becomes a house! I believe this is true.

This implies that the custom of polygamy is a slight on God's concept of marriage. God's original design is for a man and a woman to come together in holy matrimony. In Africa, a wife is often traditionally regarded as a glorified slave, while the husband is a 'god' of some sort. Perhaps this is why some unbelieving men go for more than one wife. This may find justification in culture, but not in the Word of God. Pre-marital sex, pregnancy and childbirth **before** marriage is contrary to God's concept of marriage as well.

Two Become One

In God's concept of marriage, a man and a woman are to become one.

This is a heavenly arithmetic: Oneness of the couple spells unity. The force of unity is a powerful one. Even after creation, God *"...called their name Adam..."* (Genesis 5:2). It was Adam who called His wife Eve. This will tell you how important this oneness is. It has a lot of advantages if couples practise it.

This unity is supposed to affect all realms—spirit, soul and body. Spiritually, they should belong to the same spiritual kingdom. In the realm of the soul, they should be able to think and speak in one accord. Physically, they should be able to freely share their bodies together. These make for perfect union.

The importance of the concept of oneness in marriage cannot be over-emphasized. The Bible declares that it is good and pleasant for brethren to dwell together in unity (Ps.133:1). If it is good for brethren to dwell together in unity, it is certainly more so for a couple to be united. When unity exists between a couple, tremendous power is made available and the impossible becomes possible to them.

There is a fascinating story to this effect in Genesis 11:1-9. The people were one, and had one language.

That means that they were united. They purposed to build a tower and a city that would reach heaven. Because of their oneness, even though it looked like an impossible task, God Himself acknowledged possibility.

> *And the Lord said, Behold, the people is one, and they have all one language; and this they begin to do: and now nothing will be restrained from them, which they have imagined to do.*
>
> Genesis 11:6

This is the force of unity at work. If a couple is truly merged in the spirit, soul and body, nothing will be impossible unto them. It is the original concept of God in marriage that couples enjoy the benefits of oneness. The concept of oneness teaches the believer so many lessons:- Firstly, if you are truly one with your spouse, you will treat him/her as yourself.

> *For no man ever yet hated his own flesh, but nourisheth and cherisheth it...*
>
> Ephesians 5:29

If you, for any reason, hate your spouse, it is a sign that you are not united with him/her. Whatever you cannot do to yourself, you will not do to your spouse. An understanding of this will chase away selfishness from homes. It will put an end to fightings and misunderstanding.

Secondly, the concept of oneness will make it easy for a husband and a wife to share their bodies freely with one another. It will also make it possible to derive a greater degree of pleasure from their physical union, which is their procreative power. If this concept is understood and followed, it will reduce the problems experienced in homes today.

A lady once said that man's procreative power is only meant for childbearing. She could not accept that it is also to be enjoyed. All efforts to make her understand and believe this proved abortive. Shortly afterwards, she discovered that her misconception and attitude had driven her husband to start flirting with other women. Give no place to the devil.

Thirdly, the concept of oneness teaches that divorce is not part of God's programme for the home. The husband in the home is likened to the head, while the wife is likened to the body. Even in the physical, you don't separate the head from the body, or else it will result in death. *"...And they twain shall be one flesh..."* (Matt.19:5-6). God's concept is that you do not put asunder what has been joined together.

Jesus was teaching on the subject of divorce in Matthew 19:3-12. In verses 5-6, He particularly noted that no one should put asunder what God has joined together. That has an added implication that the couple should not put themselves asunder as well.

The pharisees were puzzled at Jesus' stand on the subject of divorce. They could not reconcile that teaching with what Moses said. So they asked Him to explain why Moses asked men to write a bill of divorcement, if they choose. His answer is revealing:

> *He said unto them, Moses because of the hardness of your hearts suffered you to put away your wives: but from the beginning it was not so.*
>
> Verse 8

There must be a recourse to the beginning to understand what the truth is. The truth as revealed by God is that couples should stay together, once pronounced married.

Apostle Paul who also taught on this subject, clearly establishes God's mind on divorce.

> *And unto the married I command, yet not I, but the Lord, Let not the wife depart from her husband:*
>
> *But and if she depart, let her remain unmarried, or be reconciled to her husband: and let not the husband put away his wife.*
>
> I Corinthians 7:10-11

Notice that this is a direct command from the Lord.

This commandment stems from the fact that when God was designing marriage in the beginning, He did not consider divorce as an option. Paul employs some words—'if', 'but'—to explain some grounds for divorce. These words in their meaning show that divorce is an exception, and every possible step must be taken to guard against it.

Are you for any reason considering divorce as an option right now? Hold it a bit! Do you know that anyone that has gone through divorce will tell you that it is not an interesting experience? Even when the wounds of divorce is healed, the scar remains as long as the individual concerned is alive. Therefore, why not believe God for a miracle? God can do it! He has done it for others.

There is a couple that got married some years ago. They were married for over 10 years, but there arose a problem in their home which resulted in a divorce. At that time, both of them were unbelievers, but God did a miraculous thing in their lives. After sometime, they both became Christians, and after being divorced for about five (5) years, they are now happily reunited. God is no respecter of persons. What He has done for them, He can do for you too. Believe God for a miracle! Yours will be the next testimony!

Maturity

In God's concept, marriage is for men and women, not for boys and girls. *"...the rib, which the Lord God had taken from man, made he a woman, and brought her unto the man"* (Gen. 2:22). *"Therefore shall a man...cleave unto his wife: and they shall be one flesh"* (Gen. 2:24). Take particular note of these words 'man' and 'woman' in the above passages.

Maturity is required before marriage. One needs to be matured spiritually, physically and emotionally . However, maturity can be determined from two viewpoints: age and ability to handle life situations. These two put together, help in determining how matured an individual is. One that is mature for marriage should be able to assume responsibility for his/her actions, and take up the welfare of his/her spouse and children. If you are not mature enough to be a parent, then you are not mature enough for marriage. Adulthood is a basic requirement for success in marriage.

You will discover, therefore, that God's concept of marriage is quite different from man's concept. Everybody has a choice to make—whether to accept man's concept or God's. However, it should be noted that God, who is the sole designer of marriage, has the correct view. His view must be taken, if we desire reap the full reward of marriage.

Chapter 6

Purpose Of Marriage

God is a God of purpose. There are reasons for everything God created. His purposes are revealed to us in His Word. At creation, God did not waste time creating any worthless thing. He was judicious. Thus, marriage, which was instituted by God, is not worthless; it was intended to fulfil certain functions. The success of any marriage is determined by how well the couple align themselves with the purposes of God in this regard. In this chapter, we shall be examining some of the purposes of God for marriage as revealed to us in His Word.

1. To Provide A Helpmate

And the Lord God said, It is not good that the man should be alone; I will make him an help meet for him.

Genesis 2:18

From that scripture, it is evident that the primary purpose of marriage is to provide a help meet for man. Before Eve was given to Adam, certain responsibilities had been committed to him. It was his duty to dress and keep the garden (Gen. 2:15). But God saw that he needed help to fulfil these responsibilities.

The purpose of God in marriage is to create a help that is suitable, adaptable and complementary; not just any kind of help—a helpmate for all areas of life. Marriage is meant for improved living. The family is meant to provide help, not to establish hurt. Contrary to God's purpose, many homes today are hurting. An understanding of God's purposes for marriage will go a long way in alleviating such hurts.

2. Spiritual Reinforcement

Marriage is supposed to provide an additional strength spiritually, to make the human family an unbeatable team and establish each as partner gods of the earth. When a structure is reinforced, for instance, it is given added strength to make it stand firm, irrespective of the turbulence of the rain and the tide. It is the same thing with marriage.

This kind of spiritual reinforcement makes for spiritual prosperity. The physical world answers to the spiritual world, so spiritual prosperity will find expression in the physical too. In III John 2, John expressed a divine will there. He says:

Beloved, I wish above all things that thou mayest prosper and be in health even as thy soul prospereth.

It is evident here that God wants His people to have all-round prosperity, beginning from the spiritual. It is a spiritual law that the extent to which you prosper physically determines the extent to which you prosper in your soul. God intends the married to reinforce, support and uphold each other to find spiritual prosperity; and as they do that, they will also find prosperity in health, finances and materials.

This is not to say that Christians who are not married are necessarily weaklings, but when a man is united with God's choice for him, they become resources of inspiration to each other for soaring higher in the realm of the spirit. They become fortified and stronger.

Iron sharpeneth iron; so a man sharpeneth the coun-
tenance of his friend.

Proverbs 27:17

The purpose of God in marriage is for a man and his wife to sharpen each other. Note that only iron sharpens iron. Wood cannot sharpen iron. This reinforces the importance of the two belonging to the same kingdom spiritually.

Reciprocal reinforcement among couples makes it easy for both of them to win spiritual battles.

> *Two are better than one; because they have a good reward for their labour.*
>
> Ecclesiastes 4:9

The closest association you can find between two individuals is between a wife and a husband. When they come together and agree, sharing a common goal and living a common life, they can easily win all life's manifold battles. In God's own scheme, one will put a thousand to flight and two will chase ten thousand (Deut. 32:30).

Marriage Doesn't Make You Less Spiritual

Some people say that Christians go cold when they get married. There is no scriptural basis for this. There might be those who become less spiritual after marriage, but there are several others whose strength has more than doubled as a result of their being married. Marriage is not meant to pull you down spiritually, but to bring about spiritual uplift.

All through scriptures, you will discover that two are always better than one. When Jesus was to send His disciples on their first missionary trip, He sent them two by two. Realizing the potent force of agreement, He taught His disciples that:

> *If two of you shall agree on earth as touching any-thing that they shall ask, it shall be done for them of my father which is in heaven.*
>
> Matthew 18:19

Nowhere can the prayer of agreement work faster than in marriage. It is easier for a couple to agree on scriptural principles, than to find an outsider to agree with. Couples can take advantage of this scripture and use if for spiritual enrichment. This means that God wants married partners to be stronger for Him and not weaker.

On any issue of life, including marriage, there are always two reports: the negative report and the Biblical, positive report. Those who say that marriage reduces spiritual effectiveness have a negative report. You have a choice to make. Marriage doesn't make you less spiritual, rather, it should make you more spiritual. Ever before I got married, I discovered and chose the good report of the Bible concerning marriage. I agreed with the Word and purposed in my heart that I was not going to become less useful for Him; rather, I shall be more useful for Him and God has been faithful.

I have been married for over a decade now and blessed

with four children; yet my husband and I are still full of zeal, serving the Lord with the whole of our lives. Each new day opens with a new determination to climb higher heights. The secret is that I discarded the unscriptural idea that marriage makes you less spiritual and embraced the scripture that says, *"Two are better than one..."* You can do the same. God is no respecter of persons. You have to decide whether you will allow your marriage to weaken your faith or to invigorate you unto higher calling and service unto God.

3. Companionship

It is God's intention that marriage should offer companionship. The composition of man is such that requires constant fellowship. Loneliness has been discovered to be one of the causes of mental retardation and suicide in many. Marriage is therefore a means of fulfilling the need for fellowship.

After creation, there was only one thing God said was not good: that the man should be alone (Gen. 2:18). God rectified the only omission in the whole of creation by making a woman for the man, thereby instituting marriage. If it was not good to be alone that time, it is even more so today.

God who said it is not good for the man to dwell alone knew better. He is not dwelling alone by Himself.

For instance, He is constantly enjoying the fellowship of God the Son, God the Holy Spirit and an innumerable company of angels. This type of fellowship has been extended to man through the institution of marriage.

It is unfortunate that many couples are missing out on this purpose for marriage. Even though some couples dwell together under the same roof, constant quarrels and rancour pull them kilometres apart; so they live together but yet alone. Such marriages are always empty, a pointer to frustrations and possible divorce. This is not the will of God. God expects you to have sweet communion, not only with Him, but with your partner also. As a matter of fact, it is difficult to enjoy fellowship with God when your fellowship with your spouse is disrupted.

True companionship will add meaning to your marriage. Your spouse is not just to be your roommate, but your closest friend. Your spouse ought to be your best consultant and closest associate in all things. When this happens, you will find pleasure and fulfilment in your marriage relationship.

4. Procreation

Marriage is for procreation. The human race is being maintained through marriage.

And God blessed them, and God said unto them, be

fruitful, and multiply and replenish the earth, and subdue it...

Genesis 1:28

Here, it is worthy of note that the power to produce after their kind was transferred to the man and the woman.

This power can be rightfully exercised only in the context of marriage.

A. Planning—A Necessary Requirement

Although God commanded man to be fruitful and multiply, it is good to note that that commandment was not given only to a select few; it is for the entire human race. You are therefore not expected to keep bearing children without control. Wisdom is required in this respect. It calls for adequate, sensible planning. In as much as God wants you to have children, wisdom demands that you bear just the number you can adequately bring up in the fear of the Lord.

It is the responsibility of parents to rear children, not just to bear them. It is therefore proper for couples, even before marriage, to decide on the number of children they desire to have and plan how to space them. Some parents, especially women, have been unnecessarily worn out through childbearing. They look haggard and pitiable, because they keep having children year after year. To such women, children which are meant to be a blessing from God have become a burden. Their condition makes it difficult for them to devote time to the things of God. Such couples could have been saved from such experiences had they introduced caution, wisdom and planning.

Financial prosperity is not a justification for having too many children. This is simply because money is not the only thing you need to train children. Personal attention to each child is crucial, if they will grow up in the fear of the Lord. You also need time to pray with, and for them. You need to pay attention to yourself and your God also. All these require time. When you are choked up by excessive cares, you will throw all these essentials overboard to the detriment of your soul and that of your entire family.

Although the Word of God did not specify the number of children that a couple can have, wisdom is profitable to direct. After settling with the number of children you desire to bear, you have a wide range of control and spacing methods at your disposal, make a suitable choice for yourself after seeking medical advice.

B. A Word on Barrenness

The instruction given in the beginning to be fruitful and multiply has a major implication, and that is the fact that God has given man the ability to multiply. The scripture is very clear on this subject *"Thou shall be blessed above all people: there shall not be male or female barren among you, or among your cattle"* (Deut. 7:14). *"There shall nothing cast their young, nor be barren, in thy land..."* (Ex. 23:26). These two scriptural witnesses are unequivocal. God wants everyone to be fruitful. If there be any case of barrenness, it is certainly not from God. God did not create you barren. You were complete at creation and God said you were very good. If man calls you barren, God does not; He can heal you and He wants to. All cases of barrenness in the Bible were healed, except Michal's David's wife, who was cursed for scorning her husband. Barrenness is a curse, but thank God that Christ has redeemed us from the curse of the law. In case you have difficulty in childbearing, there are certain steps you need to take.

i. Accept What God's Word Says About You

If you find it difficult to bear children, find out what God's Word says about you, accept it, and walk in it. After creation, God said that everything He created was very good—including you. Man may call you barren but God does not. He can heal any case of barrenness, because with Him all things are possible. If there is anything missing in you (medically speaking) that is responsible for it, the devil is the thief that stole it. But you can catch the thief and recover your goods from Him. Realize that every situation is subject to change, only the truth abides.

ii. Catch The Thief

The devil is the thief. *"The thief cometh not, but for to steal, and to kill, and to destroy..."* (John 10:10). But you can catch him and make him pay back sevenfold. You catch him by rebuking him over your life and family. Command him to take his hands off your life. Resist him steadfastly in the faith and lay hold on your blessings.

iii. Make Your Request Known to God

Go to God in prayer and tell Him what you want. Ask Him to fulfil His Word on fruitfulness in your life; tell Him you receive the blessings in Jesus' name. This has to be a conscious effort of the will, for it is one thing to be given a gift, it is quite another to receive or accept it. Accept what God has provided, and give Him thanks for it.

iv. Think, Talk and Act Positively

Think as someone that has children already. When the devil comes to you with negative thoughts, wanting to make you accept the falsehood that you are barren, resist him. As a man thinks in his heart, so is he. Guard your heart with all diligence. Learn how to talk and act victoriously. Your positive confession and actions will bring God's blessings within easy reach, faster than you can imagine.

There was a lady, who had been married for about 18 years but was childless. She approached my husband for counselling and prayer. After prayer, my husband told her to think, talk and act as one who is fruitful and not barren. He told her to go to the market and buy baby things in anticipation of her baby, and that when people see her and ask her, she should be bold to tell them that the items are for the baby she was expecting. She did exactly that.

Child-like faith produces outstanding results. At the turn of the year, this lady was back with a baby as a living testimony. Don't be afraid of what people have said to you, or what they will say when you start taking some steps of faith. It is not what people say that matters, but what God says. You should be bold to declare what God says about you. Yours will be the next testimony!

5. Purity

Another purpose of marriage as seen in the scripture is to check sexual impurities.

Nevertheless, to avoid fornication, let every man have his own wife, and let every woman have her own husband.

I Corinthians 7:2

God made man with certain basic physiological needs. One of these is sexual needs. But in satisfying this urge, it ought to be done decently and in order—in the context of marriage. When sexual urge is satisfied in extra-marital context, it is contrary to God's nature and what He has ordained. Such acts will be greatly punished with His Holy indignation.

God knew that not all men will be able to live a successful holy life, without satisfying this biological need. Marriage therefore comes in handy to meet this need, and at the same time, makes it easy to live a holy life. This is not to suggest that marriage is for people who cannot control themselves. The truth is that,s if you cannot tame your sexual drive while single, you probably will not be able to exercise control when you are married. That means you will be in serious temptation when your partner is not available. Self control is a must, especially for the singles. The Holy Spirit is always available; through Him you can subdue the wild demands of the flesh.

However, God expects married couples to give sexual satisfaction to each other. Sex, in the context of marriage, is not dirty or sinful as some would have us believe. It is a creation of God and ought to be received for marital enrichment. As we noted earlier on, marriage is a union of spirit, soul and body of any couple. It is therefore not complete when the physical or bodily aspect is missing. Sexual union between couples is not just a physical act; it is symbolic of the oneness of the spirit and the soul, and of the mutual submission which God ordained.

Seen in this context, it is not scriptural to hold back from your partner with whom you are lawfully joined in marriage. Some use this to punish their partners or to press for some things. The Word of God is against this practice.

> *The wife hath not power of her own body, but the husband: and likewise also the husband hath not power of his own body, but the wife.*

> *Defraud ye not one the other, except it be with consent for a time, that ye may give yourself to fasting and prayer; and come together again, that Satan tempt you not for your incontinency.*

> I Corinthians 7:4-5

That scripture leaves no room for doubt on the ideal sexual relationship between couples. They are to enjoy each other, except they need special time for prayer. Of course, they have to reach a consensus before they embark on such action. Paul was quick to add that after such time of prayer, they should unite again so as not to give room to temptation. It means that those who withhold their bodies unnecessarily from their partners are courting trouble.

A woman was reported to have always been giving excuses each time her husband approached her. When the situation persisted unabated, the man went outside the matrimonial home to look for satisfaction. Before God, the man has no justification for his actions. But we can say the woman was responsible for his plight. She helped the devil to push her husband into sin. There was another woman whose response to her husband was equally as cold. Her husband had to resort to the filthy practice of masturbation. That was the beginning of crisis in that home.

Time spent on physical union in marriage is indeed very small. But without it, marriage is incomplete. Problems in this area have spelt doom for many homes. This is a very sensitive area and should therefore be given its rightful place.

I have addressed this portion to the married only. Sexual union is not for the unmarried. When it is engaged in outside wedlock, it is sinful, and sinners will not go unpunished. The memory of such immoral practices are often traumatic at a future date. Those who engage in it might find it difficult later in life to adjust and enjoy this God-given blessing of sex. We will return to this issue later in the book.

PART III

Chapter 7

How To Find A Marriage Partner

Whoso findeth a wife findeth a good thing, and obtaineth favour of the LORD.

Proverbs 18:22

Anyone who is considering7 marriage is required to take some steps in locating a partner. There is a need for finding. God has made some spiritual tools available for this purpose. These tools are found in His Word. For something to be found, it has to be looked for. In other words, there must of a necessity, be a seeking before a finding.

Ask, and it shall be given you; SEEK, and ye shall FIND; Knock, and it shall be opened unto you:

for everyone that asketh receiveth; and he that SEEKETH FINDETH; and to him that knocketh it shall be opened.

Matthew 7:7-8 (Emphasis mine)

The underlying prerequisite for finding is seeking. Seeking involves making a diligent search. The following steps will help in locating a partner in marriage.

1. Desire a Partner

The first step to getting a marriage partner is to sincerely desire a partner. You must be honest with yourself. What you don't desire, may not be appreciated. *"...The desire of the righteous shall be granted"(* Pro.10:24). Desires are primarily in the heart, but they eventually find expression on the outside. Admit your desire for a marriage partner privately and publicly without feeling embarrassed or ashamed. Don't pretend not to need one when you actually do. Admit it before God and man. If an occasion arises for you to declare your stand on the issue, be bold about it. "Marriage is honourable..." So note that your desire for a marriage partner is not carnal, but spiritual, if you follow God's approach to it.

2. Find Out God's Provision For Marriage In Scriptures And Appropriate It

God's Word contains all things that make for life and godliness, including marriage. When the Bible forms the foundation of your steps, you can be sure of success, because the scripture is the only sure foundation.

> **He that spared not his own son, but delivered him up for us all, how shall he not with him also freely give us all things?**
>
> Romans 8:32

God will freely give you all things, your desire about marriage inclusive. However, you need to *"Seek first the kingdom of God, and his righteousness; and all these things shall be added unto you"* (Matt. 6:33). Keep busy with the kingdom of God. Serve God with joy and gladness and with a pure heart of love for Him and then when He finds you faithful, He will add to you a partner. Hebrews 13:4 says *"Marriage is honourable..."*, so it is good. And if it is good, it must come from the Lord. James 1:17 and Romans 8:32 show that God will not withhold it from you.

3. Prayer

> **Commit thy way unto the LORD; trust also in Him; and he shall bring it to pass.**
>
> Psalms 37:5

Choosing a life-partner is crucial, it is a lifetime decision in which God's intervention is highly indispensable. A major way of ensuring God's involvement in a matter is by seeking His face in prayer.

Come to Him in prayer with an open spirit. Be confident that He loves you, He knows your end from the beginning and wants the best for you. Be specific in prayer. Tell God the kind of partner you want. Identify your God-given vision in life and ask God for a partner that will complement that vision *"...Everyone that asketh receiveth..."* (Matthew 7:8). If you ask in prayers, you will receive.

Some people express the fear that God may give them someone they do not want, when they commit everything unreservedly into His hands. So, they do not pray at all about it. This kind of thinking shows that they are not confident of God's love for them. They see God as a wicked God and are not sure of His ability to be a Father unto them.

> *If ye then, being evil, know how to give good gifts unto your children, how much more shall your Father which is in heaven give good things to them that ask him?*
>
> Matthew 7:11

No earthly parent will give a harmful thing to a child, and God is more loving than earthly parents. Be sure, therefore, that God will give you a partner after His own heart.

After you have asked in prayer according to the will

of God, refuse to doubt; rather, be confident that you have received an answer to your petition.

4. Give Thanks

...Having done all...stand!" (Eph. 6:13). How do you stand after doing all that the scripture says for you to do? Let your faith be intact and your confession fall in line. Give thanks always. If you believe that God heard your prayers, then give thanks. After giving thanks, apply patience. All these are preparations of faith and before long, you will see the manifestation.

5. Apply the 'Deep Sleep' Concept

And the LORD God caused a deep sleep to fall upon Adam, and he slept: and he took one of his ribs, and closed up the flesh instead thereof;

And the rib, which the LORD God had taken from man, made he a woman, and brought her unto the man.

And Adam said, This is now bone of my bones, and flesh of my flesh: she shall be called Woman, because she was taken out of Man.

Genesis 2:21-23

Adam needed a wife, a helpmate. God caused a deep sleep to come upon him, then He took a rib from his side with which He formed Eve. Adam was not just ordinarily asleep, but deeply asleep. Deep sleep in the sense of the Word of God connotes absolute rest, lack of anxiety and worry. Having prayed to God concerning the choice of your mate, the concept of "deep sleep" teaches that you refuse to be anxious about that situation.

6. Make Yourself As Good as the Type Of Person You Desire

The idea of "finding" a partner stresses the fact that not just anybody can be your mate. There is a "right person", who will fit-in with you, to make a complete union, which will fulfil the purpose for which God established marriage.

It is easy however, to be busy looking out for the "right person", probably laying out specific qualities to be possessed by such a one, without quite considering whether you are in a right condition to be found by another person. The all-important step to locating a marriage partner, therefore, is to make yourself as good as the type of person you desire.

Think and consider if you constitute a right person to be sought after. Do unto others as you want them to do unto you (Matt. 7:12). Remember, water seeks its own level. If you desire a pastor as a partner, you must build yourself up in the things of

God. If you desire a financial pillar for the Church of Christ as a partner, you must build yourself up to be a worthy complement.

Position yourself in God's will, purge yourself of every impurity and exhibit the qualities that you want in your mate. To find the right person, make yourself as good as the type of person you desire to have.

7. Open Your Eyes (Spiritual And Physical)

You need to make use of your spiritual and physical eyes.

Your "spiritual eyes" refers to your spirit- man and your "physical eyes" are your visible eyes, with which you see.

Open Your Spiritual Eyes

There is a need for you, after taking the preceding steps, to be vigilant and alert in your spirit. God is a Spirit and He communicates with you through your spirit. If you are not alert in your spirit, it becomes difficult, or impossible for you to catch whatever God has to pass across to you. Ensure that your spirit is devoid of rowdiness. Until your spirit catches what God has to say, you might find yourself just beating about the bush.

*The spirit of man is the candle of the LORD, search-
ing all the inward parts of the belly.*

Proverbs 20:27

God wants to give you direction, but He can only do
that through your spirit, because He is a Spirit (John
4:24). Learn to open up your spirit to hear God's
direction. Do not make the mistake of depending on
your own understanding.

To be alert in your spirit does not necessarily mean
that you should close your mouth and not talk to
anybody. You can close your physical mouth and
still be rowdy in the spirit. When your spirit is too
preoccupied, it becomes difficult to hear God speak.

*Keep thy heart with all diligence; for out of it are
the issues of life.*

Proverbs 4:23

It is your responsibility to keep your heart. No one,
not even God, can do it for you. When you keep it
diligently, you will be able to deal with the issues of
life. When you are used to receiving directions from
God on other issues of life, it becomes easy when it
comes to finding a marriage partner.

Open Your Physical Eyes

You will need to make use of your physical eyes to be
able to locate someone you can appreciate, love and

walk with for the rest of your days on earth. You must be true to yourself particularly at this stage. Some Christians think God will physically come down, hold someone by the hand and come knocking at their door to give them a partner. No! God dwells on the inside of you, if you are His child; His Spirit will minister to your spirit so you can know what steps to take.

You need to use your physical eyes to find. If you have been true to yourself all along, the Spirit of God in you will illuminate your spiritual eyes so that as soon as your physical eyes come in contact with some-one, you will know whether such a one is the right person for you or not. If that person happens to be the right one, there will be a confirmation in your spirit. If that is not the right person, the Spirit of God in you will warn you to keep off. The onus now rests on you whether to be obedient or not. But remember that to obey is safer. Don't bother yourself questioning God on whatever He tells you, it is for your own good. When He tells you not to go ahead, don't feel "led" at all to do contrary to that, or else you will reap the reward of disobedience.

Making The Move

After you have been led by the Spirit of God and you discover who your partner should be, go ahead and make it known to the person, but allow the person time to pray about it, too, and be led of God. The individual's consent is very important since walking together has to be by agreement between the two of you. If truly you have been led of God, be sure that that same God will make it known to the second party, because He is not the author of confusion.

Some men embarrass ladies with statements like "God told me that you will be my wife," "I saw you and I in a dream marching to the altar to be joined," etc. Such statements embarrass ladies and some find it difficult to even seek God's guidance. Even if God told you, or you saw the person in a dream, wisdom is needed in presentation. It is good to be simple even in presentation. This will make it easy for the other party to pray and receive God's leading.

On the other hand, some Christian ladies are often guilty of nonchalance in responding to moves made by men. It is not the best thing to do. When someone talks to you about marriage, as soon as you have an answer from God, make it known. That is wisdom.

Let me pause here to share my testimony. To the glory of God, I happen to have known God early in life. I therefore started early to pray about a life partner. I remember I specifically asked for God's will in my life and I was ready to accept His will. That was quite some years before I met my husband. After praying, I knew that God had heard and answered my prayer. I discovered that my heart was at rest. There was no anxiety or worry, though I hadn't met the person face to face and didn't know who he was.

One significant thing that I discovered after this was that for every man that came to me for marriage, the Spirit of God always immediately told me what the answer was. So, I just gave them the answer without wasting time. I thank God, because this saved me the trouble of entering into courtship that was not in His will. I was constantly open to the Spirit of God and whatever He told me, I did. I had peace in my heart.

At the time I met my husband, ever before he spoke to me, the Spirit of God in me gave me a witness, and I knew I was going to get married to him.

However, I decided to wait until he made the move. When he came to me the language was such a simple one, spoken in wisdom: "Would you want to marry me? Do you think we can go into marriage together? Why not pray about it and let me know what your answer is?", he said. Can you imagine what kind of joy filled my heart that day? After sometime, I gave him my answer and that was how our courtship started.

87

Throughout the courtship, I never had any thought contrary to the fact that we were going to have a successful home. We have been married for years now and with four wonderful children; yet, our path, even in the home, has been shining brighter and brighter. There has been no cause for regret at all. To God be the glory!

Somebody might want to ask whether it is wrong for a woman to approach a man first. As far as the scripture is concerned, it is not wrong. For "Whosoever finds a wife finds a good thing," and I believe whosoever finds a husband, too, finds a good thing. I decided to find in the spiritual but left the (initial) approach in the physical to my husband. After all, God says He will grant me the desires of my heart.

My not making the proposal gave me double assurance that God was in it and at the same time earned me the kind of respect I wanted. It is not wrong scripturally for a woman to make the proposal, but it may not be advisable.

Prerequisites For Choosing

There are some things that need to be taken into consideration in choosing a marriage partner. Some of them are:-

i. New Birth

In choosing a husband or wife, you must ensure that such a one is BORN AGAIN. The individual must have accepted Jesus Christ as Lord and Saviour. II Corinthians 6:14-16 says,

> *Be ye not unequally yoked together with unbelievers: for what fellowship hath righteousness with unrighteousness? and what communion hath light with darkness?*
>
> *And what concord hath Christ with Belial? or what part hath he that believe with an infidel?*
>
> *And what agreement hath the temple of God with idols? for ye are the temple of the living God; as God hath said, I will dwell in them, and walk in them; and I will be their God, and they shall be my people.*

The Christian is referred to as light, while the unbeliever is referred to as darkness. There is no way light and darkness can stay in the same place at the same time. If light and darkness cannot dwell together, how do you suppose that a Christian and an unbeliever can go into marriage together and expect success? It is not practicable.

Some people concluded that since they have waited for so long and have not got the right person to marry, they are ready to marry whoever comes, even unbelievers. Such people have forgotten that how long they have waited is not the important thing, but how successful the marriage they are going into will be. Take for instance, someone who is 30 years old before marriage and may probably live up to 90 years on earth. If such a person rushes into marriage with an unbeliever, it implies that he has 60 years to live with that unbeliever. The journey before him (after marriage) is longer than the one he has gone through. There is, therefore, no need to rush into a thing that will not last. Remember that God cannot forget you. He cares for you. Wait for His time.

Some young converts usually ask that if one has been in courtship before conversion, should the courtship continue after the salvation of one of the parties or not? It is so simple. When one of the parties (or both of them) gets born again, the best thing to do immediately after conversion is to break the relationship.

This is not to say that it is impossible for God to bring them together again. But even if He will, that will be later. This is because the relationship started initially when both parties were unbelievers. There was no way of knowing right from wrong, or how to follow any of the things discussed above on how to find a wife or husband. Since old things are passed away and all have become new at salvation, that kind of court-ship should be done away with.

Such individuals were in the kingdom of darkness when the relationship started, but now that one or both are saved, there is a translation into the kingdom of the Lord Jesus, which is a new Kingdom altogether. There ought not to be any carry-over from the old kingdom to the new one.

Courtship is not marriage; so a broken courtship is not divorce. It is better to break a courtship than to force things on and eventually end up with a broken home. So, at salvation, every courtship of the past must be broken. Be confident in God, He will give you a person after His heart who will be a helpmeet indeed to you.

ii. *Compatibility*

Secondly, anyone you are choosing must be one you are compatible with. Two cannot walk together except they be agreed (Amos 3:3). God will never lead you to someone that you will always disagree with. If God says two cannot walk together except they be agreed, He never will ask you to marry someone you cannot agree with.

Man is three dimensional: he is a spirit, has a soul, and lives in a body. He needs a mate who will match him in all spheres. Under the preceding sub-topic, the spiritual dimension was discussed. Let us examine the need for an individual to identify someone he can go together with in the other two dimensions—body and soul.

Physical Dimension

It is important that the person you desire to spend the rest of your life with matches your expectations in appearance and composure. This, however, must not be given undue emphasis, though it is important to choose someone you will be happy to be identified with, not someone you feel ashamed to be seen with. I wish to add that what a person looks like initially should not cloud the leading of God; people change and mature in looks and composure.

Mental Dimension

There is really no point pretending that this area is of little consequence; it is important. In the natural, it is said that water seeks its own level. So, it is essential for you to go with someone you appreciate mentally. Because we are different and have different educational backgrounds, our tastes will differ.

While choosing a partner, it should be for the purpose of marriage. Some people, even Christians, are fond of choosing for ulterior motives, not because they want to get married to such individuals. It is amazing that some people for instance, do that to get money, positions, and such like; and by the time they have fulfilled their lusts and desires, they pack it up. This is inordinate affection. Choosing should be for the purpose of marriage. Inordinate simply means "beyond proper or normal limits." It is improper to speak to someone about going out together, when you know that marriage is nowhere near your mind. As believers in Jesus Christ, we must flee youthful lusts (II Tim. 2:22), and one way of doing this is to keep oneself from every relationship that will not end up in marriage.

Chapter 8

Courtship

1. The Meaning Of Courtship

Courtship is that period between when a man and a woman agree to marry and the time they are actually joined together in marriage. A typical example of this can be found in the life of Joseph and Mary in the Bible.

Concerning the birth of Jesus, the scriptures say that Mary was espoused to Joseph. *"...a virgin espoused to a man whose name was Joseph..."* (Luke 1:27). Notice the word "virgin" in this passage. From Matthew 1:18 we also read, *"...Mary was espoused to Joseph, before they came together,..."* It is clear from these passages that there was a marriage intention between Mary and Joseph, and that they had not come together physically.

This period of courtship is of great importance and should not be toyed with. This is the time when the foundation of the home in view is laid. How well this period is handled determines, to a very great extent, how the anticipated home will be. The success or failure of the future home depends largely on what the courtship is like, just as the foundation of a house is important to the home in view. There is every reason therefore, to be spiritual about it; but if the foundation be faulty, there is nothing the righteous can do. Knowing who to marry is not the end to marriage, it is rather just the beginning.

2. Length Of Courtship

How long this period lasts varies from couple to couple. There are two schools of thought on this issue. The first say that courtship should last between three and six months. Their main reason is, "So that the devil tempt ye not." The second school of thought say that courtship must be necessarily long, a matter of many years, so that the intending couple can get to know each other properly.

But what does the Word of God say? There is no place in scriptures that says exactly how long or short courtship should be. But the Word does say that in everything wisdom is profitable to direct (Eccl.10:10). Since marriage is not a thing to be rushed into (because once you go into it, you would have to stay in it the rest of your days), it is important to be sure you know well enough who you are getting married to. Courtship should therefore be reasonably long enough, for the two individuals to get to know each other well enough, so they will be able to live together all the days of their lives. Some people have rushed into marriage, only to discover the true identity of the person they are living with, when it is too late.

A lady once came to me to inform me of her marriage intentions. I wanted to find out a few things from her, so I booked an appointment with her. It happened that the appointment could not hold, and the next time I met her, she was already married. The look on her face showed that she needed help. I later discovered that the man she married had been living outside the country for many years and had just come back; so they did not really know each other. She, of course, was in a hurry to get married, so she could travel abroad with him.

While there is nothing wrong with a woman wanting to travel with her husband after marriage, there is everything wrong in wanting to marry a man just because you want to go outside the country with him. The man, I guess, knowing himself and his spiritual limitations tried to delay the marriage, but she succeeded in convincing him, since she was ready to shoulder all the expenses. As soon as the marriage was conducted, she discovered the real nature of the man she had married. He was just not interested in the things of God. She wanted to call it quits, but God would not permit it.

The root cause of the problem was that they did not know each other well enough before marriage. If that lady had been patient enough for some months, she would have seen the true colour of the man and would have been able to decide what to do. It can be very dangerous not to know the one you are going to spend the rest of your life with. Although there is no specific time stated in scriptures, it is wise to ensure you know your fiance/fiancee well enough before going into marriage.

3. Purpose Of Courtship

Courtship period is a period of getting to know each other better. It is a time of getting to know about each other's family. There is no point hiding facts that will be useful to the other party, during this time. Any information that you know if discovered after marriage, may get the other party discouraged about continuing with you, should be made known prior to the wedding. The courtship period is a time of building a strong foundation for the home in view. The importance of this period therefore cannot be over-emphasized.

Every opportunity to attend Church meetings, fellowships and healthy social gatherings, should be exploited to enhance acquaintance for maximum benefits.

At this stage, if it is discovered that the person you are courting is not the type of person you can spend the rest of your days with, wisdom demands you call it quits.

4. Engagement

This is the formal, public introduction of each other to parents, friends and relations. It is still part of the period of courtship, but at this time the courtship is almost tending to marriage. This normally follows a successful period of courtship, when the intending couple are satisfied with each other and are sure that they can live together happily. Engagement is a way of making marriage intentions known to parents and friends. This, however, does not take the place of marriage in any way.

Engagement is also the stage at which the dowry or bride-price is paid to the parents and relations of the woman by the would-be husband. This is supposed to be a demonstration of love to the relations. When you read Genesis 24, you will discover that dowry was paid on Rebekah before she was allowed to go ahead and marry Isaac.

Whatever thing is presented for dowry must be things that are precious, not things that are contrary to the Word of God, not sinful things. These things ought to be given willingly. Genesis 24:53 says, *"And the servant brought forth jewels of silver, and jewels of gold, and raiment, and gave them to Rebekah: he gave also to her brother and her mother precious things."* Notice the words "precious things."

Some believers think and make others believe that payment of dowry is wrong and unscriptural. This is not so. From the example of Rebekah, it is scriptural to pay dowry. However, it should be noted that while it is scriptural, the things you are offering should be precious, not things that will dishonour God.

5. A Word On Virginity

Virginity can be defined as the state of being a virgin. Who is a virgin? One who has never had sexual intercourse before marriage. The Bible discusses in detail the need for both man and woman to preserve themselves before marriage. Deuteronomy 22:20-21 says:

> *But if this thing be true, and the tokens of virginity be not found for the damsel:*
>
> *Then they shall bring out the damsel to the door of her father's house, and the men of her city shall stone*

her with stones that she die: because she hath wrought folly in Israel, to play the whore in her father's house: so shalt thou put evil away from among you.

Losing one's virginity before marriage is abominable to the Lord. In case anyone ever lost his virginity before being born-again, such a one should not allow the memory of the past to rob him of the peace he should be enjoying in the home (II Corinthians 5:17).

Nevertheless, it must be mentioned that when God was looking for someone through whom to bring Jesus into the world, he sought for a virgin. Matthew 1:23 says;

Behold, a virgin shall be with child, and shall bring forth a son, and they shall call his name Emmanuel, which being interpreted is, God with us.

We as parents have a responsibility to train up our children in the way of the Lord, to possess their bodies in purity whether male or female. This is because virginity has no replacement: once lost, it can never to re-acquired. If the children the Lord blesses us with end up being wayward, we will share in their shame.

With the AIDS scare terrorizing the world today, there is no safer precaution than choosing a life of purity and chastity. There is no medical cure for this deadly virus, and most carriers of the HIV virus don't have it written on their foreheads; prevention is indeed better than cure.

The young and unmarried must seek the Lord uncompromisingly and God will preserve the treasure He created in their bodies. With the help of the Holy Ghost, it is possible to say "No!" to premarital sex. Christian parents have a role to play in educating their children on the ills of pre-marital sex.

Even the unbelieving and sceptical world has suddenly discovered the need for purity. It realizes that the condom is limited in its ability to prevent sexually-transmitted diseases, so it has taken to the streets crying out to the young to say No! to pre-marital sex. The miseries of abortion and promiscuity can be avoided, if the world would come to accept Jesus as Lord and Saviour and accept His plan as the ideal way of dealing with AIDS.

Chapter 9

Planning For Marriage

Planning plays an important role in determining the success of the home in view. Jesus' teaching in Luke 14:28-32 brought out the importance of planning.

For which of you, intending to build a tower, sitteth not down first, and counteth the cost, whether he have sufficient to finish it?

Lest haply, after he hath laid the foundation, and is not able to finish it, all that behold it begin to mock him,

Saying, This man began to build, and was not able to finish.

Or what king, going to make war against another king, sitteth not down first, and consulteth whether he be able with ten thousand to meet him that cometh against him with twenty thousand?

Or else, while the other is yet a great way off, he sen-

deth an ambassage, and desireth conditions of peace.

The phrase *"sitteth not down first"* appears twice in this passage, emphasizing the significance of the phrase. "Sitting down" in this context means planning. A good home does not drop from heaven, it is built. That is why Proverbs 14:1 says:

Every wise woman buildeth her house...

Good buildings require good planning. Just as inadequate or lack of planning in the building of a physical house affects the building at a latter date, the same way lack of adequate planning can affect the anticipated home. God is a master planner. He made the water before He created the fishes. He made the earth before He created man. Can you imagine what would have happened if the fishes were made before the water?

There are many issues that call for planning. Some of these are highlighted below.

Location (Where To Live)

After the wedding what happens? Is one of the parties going to move to where the other is or are they both going to move to a new location? You find quite a number of Christians who are undecided on what to do about this issue; so even after marriage, they still live as though they are unmarried. It is after marriage that some start planning, making it difficult to arrive at a consensus.

Finance

Another issue that ought to be discussed and settled while planning for marriage is the issue of finance. It is always safer to arrive at a conclusion on whether separate accounts or a joint account is to be kept after marriage. Finance is a sensitive issue that causes problems in some homes. One of the ways to avoid this is to arrive at a conclusion on how to do it, ever before marriage.

Number Of Children

This issue of proposed number of children is another aspect that ought to be discussed, while planning for marriage. When you bring your reasons together, it becomes easy to arrive at a conclusion. There are cases where, after marriage, one of the parties wants to have as many children as possible, while the other does not. Such things can cause misunderstanding. But it can easily be avoided through careful planning.

Vision

Issues concerning goals and plans for the future ought to be made clear to each other, while planning for marriage. It should not be after marriage before your partner begins to discover what your vision for life is. When he knows on time, he is able to decide whether he can go with you or not. When we talk about a vision, we do not mean the type received necessarily when asleep or in a trance; but a vision is the unfolding of God's plan as it concerns the individual. Every one must come to discover what plan God has for his/her future and how to arrive at that destination.

One way is to ask the Lord for a goal (vision) and then open your spiritual eyes to locate one (Matt. 7:7).

It is pathetic that a lot of people pre-occupy themselves with what to eat, drink, wear at the expense of these important issues. Christians should be able to order their priorities right.

Prerequisites For Planning

Maturity

Marriage is for men and women, not boys and girls. There is the need for maturity before anyone starts planning for marriage. Maturity is not just in age, although it is part of it, but it is maturity spiritually, emotionally, physically, etc. If you are not mature enough to be a parent, then you are not mature enough for marriage. One that is mature for marriage should be able to assume responsibility for his actions. He should be able to ensure the welfare of his mate and children. If your parents are still dictating to you, then you are not qualified to parent anyone, and you are therefore not mature enough for marriage.

Modesty

In planning for the marriage ceremony, especially with regards to entertainment and dresses, modesty is required. All things should be done to the glory of the Lord.

> *Whether therefore ye eat, or drink, or whatsoever ye do, do all to the glory of God.*
>
> I Corinthians 10:31

When you seek that His name be glorified, you will discover that He too will get Himself concerned about the affairs of your life.

Holy Spirit

Making a success of marriage requires physical stamina, love, consideration, emotional stability, and objective reasoning which come from the Holy Spirit. You must, therefore, give the Holy Spirit the room to do His work. The extent to which He is given room determines the extent to which He will operate. The Holy Spirit is the power of God. He is an enabler *"Ye shall receive power, after that the Holy Spirit is come* upon you..." (Acts 1:8). The more you give Him room, the more He enables you.

Relationship Before Marriage

Some Christians begin in the spirit and end up in the flesh. Galatians 5:19-21 lists the various works of the flesh.

Now the works of the flesh are manifest, which are these; Adultery, fornication, uncleanness, lasciviousness,

idolatry, witchcraft, hatred, variance, emulations, wrath, strife, seditions, heresies,

envyings, murders, drunkenness, revellings and such like: of the which I tell you before, as I have also told you in time past, that they which do such things shall not inherit the kingdom of God.

Some begin quite well in the spirit, but mess up half way by engaging themselves in the works of the flesh. All categories of uncleanness are referred to as the works of the flesh. Since courtship is not marriage, you have no marriage rights over the other until marriage is contracted.

The Bible says in Hebrews 13:4 that *"Marriage is honourable in all, and the bed undefiled."* Marriage is an honourable thing when the bed is undefiled. Once the bed is defiled, that marriage has lost its honour. What you do with the bed during courtship amounts to laying a foundation for what your marriage will be like when you get into it.

The law of sowing and reaping still holds here. Whilst the earth remaineth, seed time and harvest shall not cease (Gen.8:22). Since the earth is still remaining, whatever a man sows, he will reap. When the bed is defiled, the seed is sown and you can be sure that it will produce and when harvest time comes, it will manifest.

While in courtship, there is no room for sexual relationships or anything that leads to it. Somebody says, "But we intend to marry." As long as you are not yet married, it is sinful for you to go into it or do anything that leads to it. The reason why a good number of couples get involved in pre-marital sex, is heavy pettings that got out of control. Many who found themselves in it had no intention of having sexual intercourse, but one thing led to another. This is like the child who stood at the edge of a forest fire and says, "But I only lit a match." That is why the Word of God says we should abstain from all APPEARANCES of evil (I Thess. 5:22).

Don't wait until evil comes before you flee. It starts

from kisses to passionate pettings and before you know what is happening, the bed is defiled. By so doing, the seed of bitterness and problems for your future home is sown.

Some people have found themselves pregnant with babies they were not prepared for. For some individuals, the guilty feelings become barriers to adjusting in marriage. It is like a wound, even when a wound is healed, the scar is left behind.

That is why care has to be taken, so that when you begin in the spirit, you do not switch over to the flesh. The only way out is to keep walking in the spirit, for when you walk in the spirit, you shall not fulfil the lusts of the flesh.

Even if one of the partners is being tempted, the other should be able to help him overcome. It takes two to defile the bed. Daniel purposed in his heart not to defile himself (and this was under the old covenant), and he was not defiled. But we are operating under a better covenant based on better promises and it should be easier for us today to overcome, than it was in the days of Daniel.

Purpose in your heart not to defile yourself and you will not be defiled. You earn yourself respect from your partner when you marry as a virgin. Sin is deceitful; it looks sweet initially, but bites at last. Let your relationship before marriage be a holy one; that which will bring glory to God and honour to you.

This is easy as you learn to walk in the spirit.

PART IV

Chapter 10

Family Government

The family, like any other organization that involves two or more people, needs to be governed. The home has to be ruled and its affairs needs to be controlled and directed, to make for peace and fulfilment.

This responsibility for government, rests upon the shoulders of both the man and the woman in the home. This is a reason why marriage should not be entered into without consideration.

When the two parties co-operate in discharging their responsibilities, family government becomes easy and the home becomes an interesting place to live in. It becomes an abode for God and the Holy Spirit.

In this chapter, I want to discuss these responsibilities from the side of the man and that of the woman.

The Man

The Leader Of The Family Government

The man is the head and leader of the family government. *"For the husband is the head of the wife, even as Christ is the head of the Church: and He is the Saviour of the body"* (Eph. 5:23). In any human organization, there is always the need for leadership; and the home is an organization of some sort, requiring good leadership. Leadership is by no means a cheap thing. It requires strength and courage.

It is easier to be led than to lead. Men have to give leadership, not only to themselves, but also to their household. After creation, God brought Eve to Adam and presented her to him for government.

> **And the rib, which the Lord God had taken from man made he a woman, and brought her unto the man.**
>
> Genesis 2:22

The fact that God brought Eve to Adam shows that Adam had responsibilities over Eve. In fact, it was Adam that named his wife Eve (Gen.3:20). When God commanded Adam not to eat the fruit, Eve was not there. *"And the Lord God commanded the man, saying..."* (Gen. 2:16). Adam, as the leader of the family government, ought to have addressed a press conference and relayed

God's commandment to Eve. Adam failed as the leader of the family government; the devil penetrated the family, and humanity was dethroned.

God made the human family an unbeatable team and established them as gods on the earth, but because Adam failed in the family government, they lost control and were sent out of the garden of Eden.

> *Therefore the Lord God sent him forth from the garden of Eden...*
>
> Genesis 3:23

Man, if you must not suffer the kind of dethronement Adam suffered, you must have your home directly under your control.

If your family fails, it is your fault and you will be held responsible by God. After Adam and Eve ate the fruit in the garden, it was Adam that God called upon; not Eve, not the devil, but Adam (Gen. 3:9). Even though God knew that it was the devil that deceived them and gave them the fruit, which Eve ate before Adam, yet it was Adam that God called upon. Why? Because God had already committed the government of the home into his hand. If the government of your family fails, you are the one that God will call upon!

Don't make the kind of mistake that Adam made, so that you do not suffer what he suffered. *"For whatsoever things were written aforetime were written for our learning..."* (Rom.15:4). Both the man and the woman in the home must make sure that there is no communication breakdown between them.

Your placement in the kingdom of God is determined by how well you rule your home. If you cannot rule your house well, God will not allow you to rule His church, because He knows that you will not succeed at it. See what the Bible says about those to take up responsibilities in the Church.

> **One that ruleth well his own house, having his children in subjection with all gravity;**
>
> **(for if a man know not how to rule his own house, how shall he take care of the church of God?**
>
> I Timothy 3:4-5

> **Let the deacons be the husbands of one wife, ruling their children and their own houses well**
>
> I Timothy 3:12

If you can't rule your house well, there is a limit to how far you can go in the things of God. This same truth is repeated twice in the same chapter, showing its importance. How well do you rule your home?

To rule the home well, the man must be a loving leader, not a taskmaster. Love is a necessary ingredient that a man must possess for effective leadership. Christ rules the Church with the rod of love, so also for the man to succeed, he must rule his home with the same rod.

In fact, it is a scriptural commandment for the man to love his wife, as Christ loves the Church (Eph.5:25). Remember, Christ loves the Church and gave Himself for us, even while we were yet sinners. Husbands should also love their wives sacrificially, unconditionally and limitlessly. Don't forget, love is not love until it is expressed. Express your love to your wife, in words and in deed. As a woman, let me tell you one secret; no woman hates to be loved. When you demonstrate your love to your wife, you will be able to govern your home with ease.

Some men are fond of rejoicing at the fact that they are the head of the home, forgetting the responsibilities attached to that office. It is not enough to rejoice at the great authority that God has vested in the man, but to live up to the responsibilities attached to it. Anything happening to the body is felt most by the head.

Have you ever thought about that? The man occupies such a strategic position that can influence and determine what the lives of other family members will be like. As the head of the home, live up to expectation, so that Christ can be magnified, not only in your life, but in your home as well. Don't let God regret making you the head of the home!

The Welfare Of The home

The welfare of the home is committed into the hands of the man. He has to make provisions for his household. The scripture is explicit on this fact. *"But if any provide not for his own, and specially for those of his own house, he hath denied the faith, and is worse than an infidel"* (I Tim. 5:8).

The man must provide specially for his own house spiritually, materially and financially. He must ensure that his family members have what to eat and wear. Some men make provision for their village meetings, relations and friends at the expense of their immediate family members. This is contrary to scriptures.

If you don't care for the welfare of your family, the scripture says you are worse than an infidel. An infidel is an unbeliever. I know a man who cares less about providing feeding money for his family, but goes daily to eat in a restaurant. This is not scriptural and does not show that he has any love for his family.

To be able to fulfil this responsibility, the man needs to be delivered from selfishness. He must learn to have the interest of his family members at heart. My husband often says that, "Life is in phases and men are in sizes." How true that is!

You must know your size and know the phase in which your family is per time. Agree with the phase by phase lifting of your life. Eat your size, drink your size, sleep your size and wear your size. Be involved with only what you can afford as a family. Give no room to covetousness. Allow your family to grow with the uplifting grace of God. Don't destroy your tomorrow today!

Child Training

The man as the father of the children, has the responsibility of training the children. This is supposed to be done in conjunction with the wife. It is common to find men pushing the responsibility of child training to mothers. It is supposed to be jointly done by both parents. Jonadab brought up his children in the fear of the Lord and he reaped the result (Jer. 35:14, 18-19). Whatever your child becomes in life, as a father, you will partake of it whether good or bad.

Just like God as a father takes care of us, so also should fathers do all within their power to ensure that their children are trained in the way they should go, so that when they grow up they will not depart from it.

The Woman

Submission

After making the woman, God presented her to the man for government. *"And the rib, which the Lord God had taken from man, made He a woman, and **brought her unto the man"** (Emphasis mine) (Gen. 2:22).* The woman has a primary responsibility of submitting to the leadership of the man, as ordained by God from creation. It is God's command that the woman submits to her own husband. *"Wives, submit yourselves unto your own husbands..."* (Eph.5:22). It is not optional, it is an instruction.

The word "submit" means to put oneself under the control of another. A wife is therefore scripturally expected to be under the control of her husband. Woman, are you the type that your husband cannot control? Then you are not submissive!

Submission is essentially a matter of the heart, which will eventually find expression outward. So, submission affects man in his thoughts, words and behaviour. The heart is where the foundation for submission is built. Submission is not genuine when it is not from the heart; it is mere hypocrisy! Submission to one's husband should reflect in one's speech as well as in one's behaviour. Your words reveal you.

Out of the abundance of the heart the mouth spea-
keth.

Matthew 12:34

Your words reveal whether you are genuinely submissive or not. Actions, they say, speak louder than words. True submission to a husband will definitely reflect in the woman's behaviour. Notice that the submission is supposed to be "...in everything" (Eph.5:24). "Everything" covers all areas of life.

Somebody once asked, "What if a woman has an unbelieving husband, should she still submit?" Yes, because even as an unbeliever, he is still the husband. A follow-up question is: "What if the unbelieving husband wants to involve the wife in sinful acts (such as sacrificing to idols), should the woman still submit?" The answer is an emphatic No! Any submission that will make you go into sin to disobey God's Word and eventually miss heaven is unscriptural.

When whatever you do does not fit into the Lord's command as Ephesians 5:22 and Colossians 3:18 say, you are to decline. This, however, must be done in meekness.

It is important to note that submission to the man's authority, does not mean that the woman contributes nothing to the building of the home. The woman should be able to actively participate, by prayerfully making reasonable suggestions that will help their home. These ideas should be discussed by both the man and his wife in an atmosphere of love, and conclusions reached.

Arguments, fighting and disagreements should not be given room, because they are loop-holes through which the enemy might come in. In case the man is not around and decisions need to be taken, the woman should be able to adequately stand in for him. If any suggestion from either party, especially the wife's is not taken, it should be prayerfully handled. It works!

Some women prefer argument to submission in the home, thinking that by doing this they will be able to get their own way. It doesn't work that way! As a wife, there is a way you can always have what you want, if you have scriptural reasons for those desires. The weapon you need is prayer. Take your strong reasons to God in prayer and He will answer you.

There was a time my husband and I wanted to change schools for our children. There was a particular school we wanted to change them to, and we had started making arrangements for the change. But after sometime, I discovered that there was a better school they could attend.

I had my reasons, based on God's Word; one of which was that the proprietress is a spirit-filled believer and most of the workers are Christians. I told my husband about it, but he did not immediately see why I wanted that particular school, especially after both of us had agreed on one before. Because I had learnt what submission means and how to use the weapon of prayer to get whatever I wanted, instead of arguing, I took the issue to God in prayers.

I presented my reasons before God and asked Him to convince my husband Himself about the issue. God did! A few days later, my husband came home and said that that particular school I talked about was where the children would start attending! Can you imagine how excited I was that day? Immediately, all arrangements were made and they resumed there. What arguments would not have brought for me, submission and prayer did.

I believe that the problem with some people is that they think that some things are too small to pray about. God is interested in every area of your life, nothing is too small or too great to commit unto Him.

Four things that will make submission easy for you are: prayer, obedience, love and humility.

If you don't love your husband, you will find it difficult to submit to him. Women are to love their husbands (Titus 2:4). Generally, women are more susceptible to pride, and wherever there is pride, disobedience reigns and prayer cannot be effective.

Live a life of humility and obedience, then prayer will work for you and submission will also become easy for you. It's working for me, and God is no respecter of persons. I have been married for over a decade now, and my husband and I have never had any occasion to look at each other in the face, in a scuffle, argument or fight. Your submission speaks for you and wins your husband over (I Peter 3:1).

Some people think it is impossible to live together without fighting and arguing. But I am a living testimony to the fact that it is possible. If it is working for me, it will also work for you, if you believe it.

Home Maker

The woman in the home has a responsibility of making her home.

> *To be discreet, chaste, keepers at home, good, obedient to their own husbands, that the word of God be not blasphemed.*
>
> Titus 2:5 (Emphasis mine)

The home is what the woman makes it to be. An

adage says, "As you lay your bed, so you lie on it." Make your home conducive for the Holy Spirit to dwell in. There are homes you enter and you just sense the presence of the Holy Spirit. You can see joy and gladness on the faces of those who live there. There are some others that, as soon as you enter, you feel tension in the atmosphere.

The woman has a great role to play in determining the spiritual atmosphere of the home. You can determine to make your home a conducive place for the Holy Spirit to dwell in. Keep your home for Jesus, and out of the reach of the devil.

Keeping the home involves doing it physically and spiritually. Spiritually, you keep your home by prayers, the Word, fasting and watching. Physically, you keep it clean and tidy. The cleanliness in some homes commands attention, while in some others, you wonder whether cleanliness means anything to them. No matter how small or big the place you are living is, keep it clean, to the glory of God. Some women appear neat outside, but leave their homes in a mess with everything there "rioting!" This is hypocrisy. Cleanliness is part of spirituality. Woman, be clean inside and outside.

The woman, as a home keeper, prepares food for her

household. Proverbs describe the virtuous woman as one who *"giveth meat to her household"* (Pro. 31:15). Members of her household are all adequately taken care of. How well people in the home are taken care of, depends therefore on how efficient she is in performing this duty.

Keeping the home requires diligence, spiritually and physically. It is energy and time-consuming, but the result speaks for itself. A lazy woman cannot keep a home. But God will always supply the strength that is required.

Family Hospitality

The woman in the home holds the key to family hospitality. Whether a family is hospitable or not depends largely on the woman. Christians are to be hospitable, *"Distributing to the necessity of saints; given to hospitality"* (Rom. 12:13). But whether this is so or not depends a great deal on the woman. If a woman, for instance, does not want a particular guest in the house, no matter how much the man tries to cover up, it will show in his wife's reactions. The level of a man's hospitality is affected by the woman. Every woman must learn how to effectively use the key of family hospitality.

In Acts 16:14-15, there is an interesting story of a

woman called Lydia, a seller of purple, whose lifes tyle of hospitality, led her to host the apostles.

Child Training

The woman, as a mother, has duties towards her children. She has to bring up her children in the way of the Lord.

Train up a child in the way that he should go...
Proverbs 22:6

This is a commandment from God, which is not optional. Training the child includes satisfying his spiritual, physical and social needs.

For child training to be effective, a mother must love her children. It is a commandment in scriptures for mothers to love their children. Are you surprised? Don't be, because with some mothers, you can read hatred in their words and behaviour towards them. Christian parents ought to demonstrate love to their children, just like God does to His children.

Both the man and the woman have responsibilities to perform, in order to keep their home in shape. Failure of one or both of them in discharging these responsibilities is often the root cause of marital problems.

If one of the parties fails in performing his/her duties, the other party should not use that as an excuse for failing in his/her duties also. As you keep on faithfully performing your own duties, God will definitely perfect every other thing that concerns you.

Fulfil your own part of the responsibilities and family government will become an exciting thing.

Chapter 11

Child Training

Train up a child in the way he should go: and when he is old, he will not depart from it.

Proverbs 22:6

One of the privileges God has given to man is to bring offspring into the world. But as in other cases, responsibilities go hand-in-hand with privileges. So parents are not just to bring children into the world, they are also to rear them; they should not only nurse, but also train them in the fear of God.

What Child Training Is

God instructs parents to train their children. Training is different from teaching. Teaching adds to the store of knowledge, through instructions and information. But that does not mean the knowledge acquired is being used. Training, on the other hand, does not only involve teaching, but also practice. Put differently, teaching is theory, whereas training is the application of theory or knowledge, through exercise, in the day-to-day life.

To train a child therefore means to make him know correct precepts, and ensure that the precepts are followed. The objective of training is to make the child conform with God's standard of moral behaviour.

Quite a number of parents only teach their children; they do not engage them in actual training. Many children can recite what they have been taught, but often times their behaviour is at variance with the teachings. The reason is that the teachings have not become part of them; therefore they depart from the teaching later in life. For good results, child upbringing should be done as specified by God, and that is by training.

The Importance Of Child Training

Child training is of utmost importance to God, parents and to the society at large. Let us examine some of the reason for this.

i. Child Training Is A Commandment

It is a commandment from God to **all** parents. *"Train up a child..."* (Pro. 22:6). A commandment is an order, an instruction that must be obeyed and carried out.

The above statement is simply an instruction from God to all parents. It is not optional, it is obligatory. God's commandments are not grievous; when He gives an instruction, it is for man's good.

If you properly train up your children, then you are being obedient to God, and on the other hand, if you do not, you are disobedient to God. Just as no earthly parent is delighted at having disobedient children, even so is God not delighted in disobedient children.

ii. Child Training Is Profitable

Child training is not just a commandment from God, it is rewarding as well.

> *If ye be willing and obedient, ye shall eat the good of the land.*
>
> Isaiah 1:19

When you obey God by training your children, you are the one to eat the fruit of it. You are the primary beneficiary. Child training is like a seed; when you sow it today, you reap the fruit tomorrow. But if you don't sow the seed today, you reap thorns and thistles tomorrow.

A trained child today becomes profitable to his parents tomorrow, while an untrained child today will bring heartache, pain and shame to his parents in the future. If you, as a parent do not want shame and heartache at old age, train up your children. Remember Eli. Nobody wants to claim to be the parent of an armed robber, but do you know that they all have parents? Can you imagine how happy Hannah was as the mother of Samuel? Or Eunice as the mother of Timothy? Can you imagine how ashamed Eli would have been as the father of Hophni and Phinehas? It is better to train up a child than to repair an adult.

iii. Children Constitute The Future Generation

Child training is important because today's children are tomorrow's generation. If children are properly brought up in the fear of God today, there will be peace and tranquillity in the society tomorrow. If children are, however, not properly trained in the fear of God, there will be corruption and heartache in the society tomorrow. The future of the society lies in the hands of parents and how they handle child training today. If you do not train your child today, you will be one of the those responsible for the corruption of the society tomorrow.

How To Train Your Child

Parents need two essential tools in order to train their children correctly and effectively. These are Love and

Control. These two go together, neither can be effective without the other. An uncontrollable child cannot be loved, neither can an unloved child be controlled.

i. Love

Christian parents should spend time with their children in the Word of God, since God Himself expresses His love for us through His word. A relationship of mutual trust should be developed with the child, so as to eliminate fear, as is the case with perfect love.

Learn to demonstrate your love to your children. Carry the young ones, hug them, buy things for them sometimes, compliment them when necessary and do not lay undue emphasis on their weak points. When you show them love, it makes it easy for them to know and understand God's nature, which is love, and walk in it.

A Christian parent should always remember that the words uttered to a child ultimately makes or destroys the child's future. Words of love, not of condemnation should be spoken to the child. The life of a child is patterned after the words his parents says to him. Training a child actually means showing him what to do by example; it means to instruct the child by practising same. It is not proper to ask a child to do what you won't do yourself. A child should be trained with tenderness and love.

ii. Control

A child cannot be effectively trained without control; that is, control on the part of both the parent and the child. The child is not supposed to control his parents. There are homes where the child dictates to the parents; where for instance, the child dictates the menu, whether to go to school or not, where daddy and mummy should go, and so on.

Before long, the child takes control of the affairs of the home. Parents are supposed to be in control, not the children. They have been commissioned by God to train, give direction and control children. If the excesses in a child are not controlled early in life, those excesses will later control and may eventually destroy him.

The Place Of Discipline In Training

Training involves administering discipline. Children without proper discipline are susceptible to destruction, and can bring shame to their parents.

Eli the priest showed laxity in disciplining his children. His sons defiled women in the temple, and abhorred the offering of the Lord. He failed to restrain them and this had many adverse effects. First, his family was cut off from the priesthood in Israel. Second, Eli's two sons and Eli himself lost their lives. Third, the whole land of Israel was punished: they lost the ark of God to their enemies in battle (I Sam. 4:1-11). What a price to pay for indiscipline!

Unlike Eli, however, Jonadab brought up his children in the way of the Lord (Jer. 35:14,18-19). After the death of Jonadab, his children walked uprightly before the Lord. 200 years after his death, his descendants were still following his precepts. Because of this, he found favour with God. God promised that his family will never lack a male descendant before Him.

The Rod As A Tool

The rod is a tool for discipline and control. An adage that should be considered seriously is this: "Spare the rod and spoil the child." This is simply re-echoing several admonitions in the Bible.

Withhold not correction from the child: for if thou beatest him with the rod, he shall not die.

Thou shalt beat him with the rod, and shalt deliver his soul from hell.

Proverbs 23:13-14

The rod does not kill; rather, it saves from folly and destruction.

135

However, the rod should not be the first resort. It is good only after several warnings have been issued over a particular act of indiscipline. Do not wait to see your children make mistakes in order to pounce on them with a cane. Remember that the rod is only the physical side of the spiritual tool of prayer, you must have employed in disciplining them. In other words, the rod should be complementary to prayer.

If and when the rod must be engaged, caution should not be thrown to the wind. Do not abuse the tool by over-beating your children. Lack of restraint can inflict serious injuries on your child. Recklessness in beating your child will portray you as a tyrant, in which case the child becomes hardened, instead of being disciplined.

The Place Of Prayer In Discipline

The physical world is controlled by the spiritual. Parents need to make time available to pray with and for their children. The power in Prayer can make training very easy. In prayer, you communicate with God, committing your children into His hands, moulding them up spiritually in prayer and trusting Him for excellence in their lives. Outside prayer, the rod is useless in child training.

Chapter 12

Sustaining The Christian Home

It is not enough to build a Christian home, it has to be sustained. The reason Jesus came is to give abundant life, even in the home. Man must, however, cooperate with God to make the home a mini-paradise on earth, as it is supposed to be. Whether your home is sustained or not does not depend on God, but on you. Some of the things that will help you in sustaining your home are discussed in this chapter. When you do your own part, God will always fulfil his own part.

1. Lay Your Foundation on the Rock

The foundation of a building determines to a very large extent what happens to it, and whether that building will last long or not. If something fundamental goes wrong with the foundation, very little can be done to sustain the building. It is the same thing with marriage. For your home to be sustained, you must lay your foundation upon the Rock, in the person of Jesus Christ.

How do you lay the foundation of your marriage upon the Rock? By making Jesus Christ the central focus in your home and allowing Him to take His rightful place. If you are married and you are not yet born- again, you must accept Jesus as your Lord and Saviour. If you are already born-again, whatsoever He tells you to do, do it.

> **Whosoever cometh to me, and** heareth my sayings, **and** doeth them, **I will shew you to whom he is like:**
>
> **He is like a man which built a house, and digged deep, and laid** the foundation on a rock: **and when the flood arose, the stream beat vehemently upon that house, and could not shake it: for it was founded upon a rock.**
>
> **But he that** heareth, **and** doeth not, **is like a man that** without foundation **built an house upon the earth; against which the stream did beat vehemently, and immediately it fell; and the ruin of that house was great.**
>
> Luke 6:47-49

Laying your foundation on the Rock means ruling your home with the Word of God. This is because Jesus is the Word of God (John 1:1).

How much room do you give the Word of God in your home? If you pattern your home after God's Word, then your home is built on the solid rock, and it shall surely be sustained. If your home is not built on God's Word, then it is without a foundation, and it cannot be sustained, no matter what anybody tries to do to help! "If the foundations be destroyed, what can the righteous do?" (Ps. 11:3).

Truly, the righteous can do nothing once the foundation is destroyed. Do not let the foundation of your home be destroyed. Do not attempt to run your home outside Jesus Christ and expect to make it. Jesus is the only sure foundation; lay your foundation on the solid Rock, and your home will stand.

2. Fulfil Your Marriage Responsibilities

Marriage has responsibilities attached to it. Both the man and the woman must co-operate in fulfilling their responsibilities, so that the home can be sustained. Negligence on the part of either party can affect the sustenance of the home. Co-operation therefore is a necessity. The wife, for instance, should submit to her husband in the home, be chaste, respectful and pure in her conversation. She should keep her home, making it a conducive place for the Holy Spirit to dwell.

The man on the other hand, must play a leadership role in the home, make provision for his family and train his children in the way of the Lord. When both the man and the woman play their roles well, it becomes easy for the home to be sustained.

No storm of life will be able to destabilize their home, because the force of agreement will be in operation.

In case one of the parties does not co-operate in fulfilling his/her own responsibilities, the other party should not use that as an excuse for negligence. The faithful party should fulfil his/her own part, live a life that speaks and then prayerfully seek guidance from God on how to go about carrying out other things!

3. No Hide-and-seek Game

For the home to be sustained, both the man and the woman must be open to each other. There should be no occasion to hide something from one another. *"And they were both naked, the man and his wife, and were not ashamed" (Gen. 2:25)*. The word "naked" in the above passage means 'openness' to one another. If a couple is open to each other, they will not know shame and their home will be sustained.

There are quite a number of people who hide things from their spouses, even Christians! Some believe it is an insult for a wife/husband to know their income, so they keep their money where their spouse does not know, pretending to have no money.

Even in your finances, be open! If your wife does not

know your income for instance, she may be expecting too much from you, which may cause instability in your home. When it comes to money, many believers are affected. Some hide certain information about their relations, background, plans and prospects.

Whatever information you know will make your spouse disappointed in you if he/she hears it from someone else, should be made known on time, else you are involved in a hide-and-seek game. Funny enough, whether you like it or not, it will unexpectedly be discovered one day.

Instability in some homes today was caused by certain things or information that were kept away from the other party, which were later discovered. If you do not want shame in your home, avoid playing hide-and-seek. Be straight-forward, be open!

I have never had anything to hide from my husband about myself, relations, finances, plans or anything about my life; neither does he have anything to hide from me. This has made life interesting and exciting for both of us. You can enjoy the same fulfilment in your home. I release that grace unto you and your home right now; receive it in Jesus' name.

4. Wisdom—The Principal Thing

Wisdom is the principal tool for sustenance. *"Wis-*

dom is the principal thing..." (Pro. 4:7). Both the man and woman in the home need to constantly ask God for wisdom in handling the day-to-day affairs of their home. An act of foolishness on the part of any of them, may affect the stability of the home. Wisdom tells you when to talk and when to keep quiet; what to say and the right time to say it; where to go and at what time, etc. Do you know it is possible to say the right thing but at the wrong time and thereby cause instability in your home?

> **Through wisdom is a house builded; and by understanding it is established.**
>
> Proverbs 24:3

For your home to be sustained, you need wisdom. This wisdom comes from God and whenever you need it, you can ask Him for it. *"If any of you lack wisdom, let him ask of God, that giveth to all men liberally, and upbraideth not; and it shall be given him"* (James 1:5). Whenever you are faced with a situation that requires wisdom in your home, just pray a simple prayer, asking God to give you wisdom to handle the situation, and it shall be given you. Wisdom builds and foolishness destroys.

5. Constantly Give God Glory

As you take the steps mentioned above, and enjoy

the peace and blessings of God in your home, constantly give God back all the glory. By fulfilling your own part of the covenant, you are building; but in the ultimate, God is the one building and sustaining your home for you—*"For every house is builded by some man; but he that built all things is God"* (Heb. 3:4).

That is why the Bible says: *"Without me ye can do nothing"* (Jn.15:5). All your efforts to build and sustain your home will be in vain outside God Himself. Constantly acknowledge Him as the only reason behind the sustenance of your home. Reverence and give Him His rightful place, give Him back all the glory. As you do that, He will supply you more grace and wisdom to sustain your name.

See God as the only reason behind the success of your home and He will take you to a higher realm. It works like fire! This is what my husband and I do, and it is working for us. We never attribute the success in our home to ourselves, rather, we constantly acknowledge God as the sole reason why we have enjoyed so much success and give Him back all the glory, then He makes it a better place yet!

Chapter 13

Relationship With The In-Laws

It is not God's will that anything should put your marriage asunder, not even your in-laws.

> *What therefore God hath joined together, let no man put asunder.*
>
> Matthew 19:6

The success or failure of your marriage should not be left at the mercy of extended family members. Most of the problems in the home are not directly between the wife and her husband, but between in-laws and one of the spouses.

Members of your extended family are your relations, not members of your immediate family. You need to order your priorities right. It will not be wise, therefore, to care for them at the expense of your immediate family. You should care for both of them, but one takes priority over the other. Whatever you can make available to your extended family members is a help. Your immediate family is your direct responsibility.

It is common to find men, in particular, sending money to their relations, while telling their immediate family that there is no money, not even for food. Some women, too, send money meant for feeding the family to their relations, thereby causing trouble in the home.

The Bible is clear on this subject: *"But if any provide not for his own, and specially for those of his own house, he hath denied the faith, and is worse than an infidel"* (I Tim. 5:8). Provision for your immediate family is a must.

When you get yourself too involved in extended family matters and take up their responsibilities at the expense of your immediate family, you make them shy away from their own responsibilities and they, in turn, become irresponsible. You need not carry them on your shoulders. If you do that for too long, they will not be able to develop on their own. Don't be a keeper of another man's vineyard, leaving your own untouched or haphazardly done (Songs of Solomon 1:6).

There is an account in I Kings 20:39-40 that is good for our admonition:

And as the king passed by, he cried unto the king:

and he said, Thy servant went out into the midst of the battle; and behold, a man turned aside, and brought a man unto me, and said, Keep this man: if by any means he be missing, then shall thy life be for his life, or else thou shalt pay a talent of silver.

And as thy servant was busy here and there, he was gone. And the king of Israel said unto him, So shall thy judgment be; thyself hast decided it.

The man in this story was busy in the wrong direction. He lost his life in the process. Do not be foolish like him.

Someone may want to ask whether after marriage the extended family should be forgotten completely. There is nothing to suggest this. The Bible indicates that you should not hide from your flesh; members of your extended family are your flesh that you cannot hide from (Isaiah 58:7). However, you need to order your priorities right. When you learn to order your priorities right, you will discover that things will work out without any problem. Obey what the Word says and you will have what God has promised.

Chapter 14

Getting Your Loved Ones Saved

There are quite a number of people today who were not Christians when they got married. Some of such people still have some loved ones, such as their spouses or children who are not yet in the faith. These loved ones constitute a thorn in their flesh today; and they constantly wish they will be saved also.

How would you feel when you get to heaven and see any of your loved ones in hell? How full will your joy be? It is possible for you and your loved ones to make heaven.

> *And Noah went in, and his sons, and his wife, and his sons' wives with him, into the ark, because of the waters of the flood.*

> Genesis 7:7

Noah and his household were all miraculously saved

while all others were destroyed. If Noah and his household could be delivered from the flood, you and your household can also be delivered from hell fire.

> *Believe on the Lord Jesus Christ, and thou shalt be saved, and thy house.*
>
> Acts 16:31

When it comes to salvation, a person's will is involved in accepting or rejecting Christ Jesus. But then, there are certain things you can do to get such people saved. Some of those things will be discussed in this chapter. I must say this however, that, there are no established rules in soul-winning that will work for everyone. God might lead one person in one way and another in a different way entirely. There is therefore, a need to remember the vital role of the Holy Spirit in drawing people to Christ.

> *Not by might, nor by power, but by my spirit, saith the Lord of hosts.*
>
> Zechariah 4:6b

> *No man can come to me except the Father which had sent me draw him:*
>
> John 6:44a

The Father is the one that draws people through the instrumentality of the Holy Spirit.

The following steps will help in winning your loved ones to Christ.

1. Prayer

The physical world can be controlled in the spiritual realm. Prayer changes things. In prayer, make your request known to God about such a one (Phil.4:6).

In prayer, you are not just asking that the Lord will save the individual, but you are also breaking the power of sin and death over such lives, because the devil has their minds blinded.

> *...the god of this world hath blinded the minds of them which believe not, lest the light of the glorious gospel of Christ, who is the image of God, should shine unto them.*
>
> 2 Corinthians 4:4

The devil blinds the minds of unbelievers and that is why they do not see the light of the gospel. It therefore takes a higher power to heal such minds. If you have an unsaved husband, wife or child, it is your duty to command the blindfolding of the devil to be removed.

Pray this prayer in faith because God answers only the prayer of faith. Do not doubt in your heart, refuse to be anxious about it. Ordinarily, no one in his right mind will drive his car into the gutter to kill himself, so also no one in his right mind will head for hell.

You could also pray and ask the Lord to send some-body across the path of your loved one. *"Pray ye...the Lord of the harvest, that he will send forth labourers into his harvest"* (Matt. 9:38). You can believe God for a labourer to cross your unsaved loved one's path. There is always somebody who can talk to your relative when you cannot!

Remember, your prayer must be based upon the Word of God. No prayer life is going to be successful, if it is not based on the Word of God. The manifestation of these prayers can come faster, if God's Word is strong-ly rooted in you.

Never you pray tragedies on people to make them get born- again. As you pray in faith, with your prayers based on God's Word, the spirit of conviction comes on such a one and salvation becomes easy. If your husband or wife is unsaved, use Proverbs 5:18-20 in your prayer. It says:

> *Let thy fountain be blessed: and rejoice with the wife of thy youth.*
>
> *Let her be as the loving hind and pleasant roe; let her breast satisfy thee at all times; and be thou ravished always with her love.*
>
> *And why wilt thou, my son, be ravished with a strange woman, and embrace the bosom of a stranger?*

It works like fire!

2. Fasting

You could also set some time apart to fast for the salvation of your loved one. Fasting means doing away with food for the purpose of concentration. It subdues the flesh and makes it more sensitive to God.

> *This kind can come forth by nothing, but by prayer and fasting.*
>
> Mark 9:29

Sacrifice some of your meals for the salvation of your loved one and see what God will do! Your fasting, however, must be coupled with prayer and the Word. Outside of these two, fasting is mere dieting! Your fasting must also be done in wisdom. The length of your fasting has nothing to do with its effectiveness.

I once met an elderly woman who got born again after she was married. Apparently, her husband was deep into the occult. This woman took up the challenge and started praying for her husband, breaking the power of the devil over his life. At a point in time, she started sacrificing her breakfast for her husband's salvation. According to her, she would prepare her breakfast and give it to the needy. She did this for two years!

Meanwhile, she was in a different city from where

her husband was. Unknown to her, God sent someone across the man's path and he gave his life to Christ. The next time this woman met her husband, he was born again! We serve a God of miracles! Can you imagine her joy that day? But she was patient about it. Yours will be the next testimony in Jesus' name.

3. A Life That Speaks

Your life is the greatest witness, especially to your loved ones. If you live the Christian life, it will influence your spouse, children and other relations, so that without opening your mouth to witness to them (even though it is scriptural to witness to them), they will be attracted to the kingdom of God.

Remember that old proverb, "Action speaks louder than words." There is a life that speaks! Its voice is louder than the sound from the vocal cavity of man. It gets an unbelieving wife or husband saved and draws rebellious children into the kingdom; it ministers and brings glory to God. This is the kind of life every believer must live in the home, at work, at the market place and everywhere, so that sinners can be magnetized into the kingdom of God.

Let your light so shine before men, that they may see your good works, and glorify your Father which is in heaven.

Matthew 5:16

Let Jesus, who is on your inside, speak through your life.

I have had opportunities to counsel people who have unsaved loved ones; and have come to discover that quite a number of them do not live lives that speak in their homes.

I once met a woman who was having problems with the salvation of her husband, and I discovered from my discussion with her, that the way she used her tongue in the home constituted the major obstacle to the man's salvation. Brethren, be chaste in your conversation! Women are usually guilty of this. As long as you keep nagging, your unsaved husband, wife, children, or relatives, after a while, they will not even like you being around them. This may even lead to divorce. Do not let your tongue be a trap to your loved ones; let it be an asset!

At the time I became a Christian, quite a number of my relations were not saved. I simply put the above-mentioned points to work, and today, to the glory of God, they are all Christians! Do not give up, yours in the next testimony!

Chapter 15

Homosexuality: God's View And His Remedy

The dictionary defines a homosexual as one who is sexually attracted only to people of the same sex as oneself. God defines it as an abomination. Leviticus 18:22 says: *"Thou shalt not lie with mankind, as with womankind: it is abomination"* Yet the world is teeming with homosexuals; some churches even conduct marriages for homosexuals! They are fighting for the right to be regarded as a nuclear family. They are everywhere: in government, on the streets, in institutions of learning.

Watching CBN'S 700 club one day, I saw a Christian woman who had been ensnared by the spirit of homosexuality (it's a spirit you know) and who required help to break the habit. She had suffered in secret for many years and now needed deliverance.

In secondary schools, youngsters are drawn into homosexual practices by cruel seniors, and their own lust. But for whatever reason, homosexuality is of the devil. Romans 1:26-27 (Good News Bible) reads:

Because they do this, God has given them over to shameful passions, Even the women pervert the natural use of their sex by unnatural acts.

In the same way the men give up natural sexual relations with women and burn with passion for each other. Men do shameful things with each other, and as a result they bring upon themselves the punishment they deserve for their wrongdoing.

Origin

Where did the problem emanate? From the fall. After man fell and handed the government of the world over to the devil, the devil tried to pervert every good and perfect thing God had made.

God created a means of procreation between the man and his wife. After the fall, man wondered what it will feel like to mate with animals and with people of like sex. What God created to be enjoyed between the man and his wife became marred. Man began to seek other women outside marriage; he began to crave for intercourse with men.

Unregenerated man keeps searching for new ways of living in "excitement". Because homosexuality is a spirit, they become chained to it and are unable to escape. When a man becomes born-again, something happens: sin has no dominion over him any longer (Rom.6:14). He is free to walk away, and as a matter of fact is advised to flee from every appearance of evil.

Remedy

What is the remedy for anyone caught in the web of homosexuality?

A. Become Born-Again

Only Christ has the remedy. When He died on the cross, He paid the price for all sins, once and for all (Rom.6:6). God loves you, and wants to deliver you from every trap of the devil. Homosexuality is a trap and its only recompense or reward is AIDS. Do not toy with it, come to Jesus today and He will free you from its hold.

As parents, our children must be brought up in the fear of the Lord. Teenagers need to be occupied doing positive things to create an outlet for inherent drives. We must teach our children to say a resounding No! to pressures by peers to experiment with their bodies and "discover" sensitive areas. Only Christ has the remedy.

B. Receive A New Mind

After giving one's life to Christ, if the individual has had previous homosexual experiences, another battle has to be fought and won. This battle rages on in the mind. Romans 1:28 documents God's punishment for those caught in the grip of this evil, and it affects their minds.

> *Because these people refused to keep in mind the true knowledge about God, he has given them over to corrupted minds, so that they do the things that they should not do.*

(Good News Bible)

The penalty of dabbling into homosexuality is a corrupted or reprobate mind. I suggest that the following steps be taken to disabuse the mind:

1. **Believe** that now you are in Christ, old things have indeed passed away (II Cor.5:17). Believe that God has forgiven you and forgive yourself!

2. **Read** the Bible and spend time meditating on God's Word. Memorize scriptures, and let them be a part of you (Ps.119:11).

3. **Pray**: There is no situation that prayer cannot change. Continue to 'wash' your thoughts on your knees. For effectual prayer, you need the Holy Spirit. Receive the baptism of the Holy

Spirit (Rom.-8:26).

4. **Fast**: Set time aside to wait upon the Lord in a fast and consolidate your freedom.

5. **Make Christian friends** and spend time discussing edifying things. Do not engage in idle talk.

6. **Attend a Bible Believing Church** where the mind of God is made known in unequivocal terms.

7. **Literature**: keep away from dirty novels (as long as Christ is not glorified, it is deadly) which propagate inordinate sexual acts. Keep yourself busy in the kingdom and discipline yourself. No one can reach your thoughts; so you, by yourself, must consciously guard your heart with all diligence. Philippians 4:8 has an all-purpose drug. It reads:

> *Finally, brethren whatsoever things are true, what-soever things are honest...just...pure... lovely...of good report...If there be any virtue, and if there be any praise, think on these things.*

If the steps discussed above are followed, you will receive total freedom from this deadly disease of homosexuality.

Final Word

If ye be willing and obedient, ye shall eat the good of the land.

Isaiah 1:19

It is not enough for you to just go through the materials in this book. You need to take heed to what you have read. Remember that marriage is a covenant, not a promise. You are a party to the covenant. God is also a party to it. You have to fulfil your own side of the covenant by doing whatever the Word of God tells you to do. Only those that are willingly obedient can eat the goodness of marriage.

God wants you to eat the good of the land, even in your home. He wants the best for you; but it takes your obedience. Marriage is gold, but you have to dig it up before you can enjoy it. Remember, *"to obey is better than sacrifice and to hearken than the fat of rams"* (I Sam. 15:22).

Let God turn your home around for the better, as you obey and do what the spirit of the Lord is passing across to you through this material. Be a doer of the Word, and your light will keep shining brighter and brighter unto the perfect day. A happy home is your heritage. Opt for it and your home will be heaven on earth.

ABOUT THE AUTHOR

FAITH ABIOLA OYEDEPO HAS BROUGHT HOPE, JOY, AND LIFE INTO MANY HOMES IN HER GENERATION.

Having received a ministry for family and homes, she has dedicated her life to showing people God's perfect will for their homes and family relationships. Her weekly newspaper and internet columns: Family Matters, Family Success and Family Life have helped in no small way in achieving this goal.

She has shown in practical terms and through deep spiritual insight that the home can be the Eden God created it to be.

She has a divine mandate to make her shoulders available and enrich the lives of singles in a unique way.

Pastor Faith has written more than 12 books, including: Marriage Covenant, Making Marriage Work, Raising Godly Children, and her best selling title: Rescued From Destruction.

An anointed preacher of the gospel, Pastor Faith Abiola Oyedepo has been doggedly supportive of her husband (Dr. David o. Oyedepo, the Visioner and President of Living Faith Church Worldwide Inc.) in the daunting work of the ministry.

She has four children — David Jnr., Isaac, Love and Joys.